The Cheese Book

Jean Paré

www.**companys**coming.com
visit our web-site

D0509062

Front Cover	1. Blue Cheese Pistachio Bread, page 30
	2. Burger Quiche, page 48
	3. Baked Radiatore Alfredo, page 117
	4. Feta-Stuffed Peppers, page 14

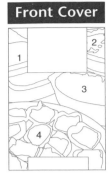

Props Courtesy Of:
Pier 1 Imports
The Bay

Back Cover	1. Chocolate Cheesecake, page 51
	2. Lemon Cheesecake, page 55
	3. Coffee Cheesecake, page 50
	4. Blueberry Cheesecake, page 57

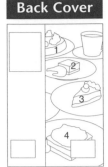

Props Courtesy Of:
Linens 'N Things
Sears Canada Inc.
Stokes

The Cheese Book
Copyright © Company's Coming Publishing Limited
All rights reserved worldwide. No part of this book may be reproduced in any form by any means without written permission in advance from the publisher. Brief portions of this book may be reproduced for review purposes, provided credit is given to the source. Reviewers are invited to contact the publisher for additional information.

Second Printing March 2002

Canadian Cataloguing in Publication Data

Paré, Jean
        The cheese book

(Original series)
Includes index.
ISBN 1-895455-89-8

        1. Cookery (Cheese) I. Title. II. Series: Paré, Jean Original series.

TX759.5.C48P37 2002   641.6'73   C2001-904235-3

Published by
COMPANY'S COMING PUBLISHING LIMITED
2311 - 96 Street
Edmonton, Alberta, Canada T6N 1G3
Tel: (780) 450-6223   Fax: (780) 450-1857
www.companyscoming.com

Company's Coming is a registered trademark owned by Company's Coming Publishing Limited

Printed in Canada

Cooking Tonight?
Drop by companyscoming.com

companyscoming.com

| Who We Are | Browse Cookbooks | Cooking Tonight? | Home |

everyday ingredients

feature recipes

feature recipes — Cooking tonight? Check out this month's *feature recipes*—absolutely FREE!

tips and tricks — Looking for some great kitchen helpers? *tips and tricks* is here to save the day!

reader circle — In search of answers to cooking or household questions? Do you have answers you'd like to share? Join the fun with *reader circle*, our on-line question and answer bulletin board. Great for swapping recipes too!

cooking links — Other interesting and informative web-sites are just a click away with *cooking links.*

cookbook search — Find cookbooks by title, description or food category using *cookbook search*.

contact us — We want to hear from you—*contact us* lets you offer suggestions for upcoming titles, or share your favorite recipes.

Company's Coming
COOKBOOKS®

everyday
recipes trusted
by millions

Company's Coming Cookbooks

Original Series

- 150 Delicious Squares
- Casseroles
- Muffins & More
- Salads
- Appetizers
- Desserts
- Soups & Sandwiches
- Cookies
- Vegetables
- Main Courses
- Pasta
- Cakes
- Barbecues
- Pies

- Light Recipes
- Preserves
- Light Casseroles
- Chicken
- Kids Cooking
- Breads
- Meatless Cooking
- Cooking For Two
- Breakfasts & Brunches
- Slow Cooker Recipes
- Pizza
- One Dish Meals
- Starters
- Stir-Fry

- Make-Ahead Meals
- The Potato Book
- Low-Fat Cooking
- Low-Fat Pasta
- Appliance Cooking
- Cook For Kids
- Stews, Chilies & Chowde
- Fondues
- The Beef Book
- Asian Cooking
- The Cheese Book
- The Rookie Cook ◄NEW►
  July 1/02

Greatest Hits Series

- Biscuits, Muffins & Loaves
- Dips, Spreads & Dressings
- Soups & Salads
- Sandwiches & Wraps
- Italian
- Mexican

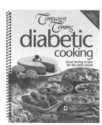

Lifestyle Series

- Grilling
- Diabetic Cooking

Special Occasion Series

- Chocolate Everything
- Gifts from the Kitchen
- Cooking for the Seasons

Table of Contents

Foreword

Appetizers

Desserts

Salads

Soups

Cheese Index

Reader Survey

The Company's Coming Story

Jean Paré grew up understanding that the combination of family, friends and home cooking is the essence of a good life. From her mother she learned to appreciate good cooking, while her father praised even her earliest attempts. When she left home she took with her many acquired family recipes, a love of cooking and an intriguing desire to read recipe books like novels!

"never share a recipe you wouldn't use yourself"

In 1963, when her four children had all reached school age, Jean volunteered to cater the 50th anniversary of the Vermilion School of Agriculture, now Lakeland College. Working out of her home, Jean prepared a dinner for over 1000 people which launched a flourishing catering operation that continued for over eighteen years. During that time she was provided with countless opportunities to test new ideas with immediate feedback—resulting in empty plates and contented customers! Whether preparing cocktail sandwiches for a house party or serving a hot meal for 1500 people, Jean Paré earned a reputation for good food, courteous service and reasonable prices.

"Why don't you write a cookbook?" Time and again, as requests for her recipes mounted, Jean was asked that question. Jean's response was to team up with her son, Grant Lovig, in the fall of 1980 to form Company's Coming Publishing Limited. April 14, 1981, marked the debut of "150 DELICIOUS SQUARES," the first Company's Coming cookbook in what soon would become Canada's most popular cookbook series.

Jean Paré's operation has grown steadily from the early days of working out of a spare bedroom in her home. Full-time staff include marketing personnel located in major cities across Canada. Home Office is based in Edmonton, Alberta in a modern building constructed specially for the company.

Today the company distributes throughout Canada and the United States in addition to numerous overseas markets, all under the guidance of Jean's daughter, Gail Lovig. Best-sellers many times over in English, Company's Coming cookbooks have also been published in French and Spanish. Familiar and trusted in home kitchens around the world, Company's Coming cookbooks are offered in a variety of formats, including the original softcover series.

Jean Paré's approach to cooking has always called for quick and easy recipes using everyday ingredients. Even when traveling, she is constantly on the lookout for new ideas to share with her readers. At home, she can usually be found researching and writing  recipes, or working in the company's test kitchen. Jean continues to gain new supporters by adhering to what she calls "the golden rule of cooking": never share a recipe you wouldn't use yourself. It's an approach that works—*millions of times over!*

Foreword

Adding cheese to your everyday cooking can bring a world of taste to your table. New varieties are always popping up at the grocery store as North Americans continue to seek out fresh and exotic tastes from other countries.

Cheese courses are becoming popular again and are often served just before, or during, dessert. Hosting a wine and cheese party is a great way to sample a selection of cheeses before deciding on favorites.

As an ingredient, many cheeses continue to be popular because they are easily melted, crumbled, roasted, broiled, baked and deep-fried. They can add texture, color and, of course, flavor to your dish. Experiment with a different cheese and you have a new taste twist on a classic recipe.

The varieties of cheese to choose from can be intimidating—there are, after all, more than 2000 different kinds of cheese worldwide. The *Glossary of Cheese*, pages 10 and 11, describes over 30 popular cheeses that were used in this book. On pages 8 and 9 you will find tips on how to buy, store, cook and serve cheese as well as a *Cheese Substitution Chart* to help you mix and match cheeses.

Nutritionally, cheese continues to be part of a healthy, and very tasty, diet. Actual fat content in cheese is lower than you might expect. At the same time cheese remains high in protein, calcium, phosphorus and vitamin A and is lower in lactose than milk. If fat intake is a true concern, look for lower-fat (light) cheese varieties.

Get ready to sample the piquant taste of Blue Onion Pie, Vermicelli Plate With Myzithra or Cheese Sticks. You'll marvel at how Asiago cheese breathes new life into traditional grilled cheese sandwiches and

appreciate Coffee Cheesecake, not only for its delicious taste but also because it's made with light and non-fat cream cheese.

The Cheese Book offers you over 140 different ways to enjoy cheese, so add a few new kinds of cheese to your grocery list. Everyone will be surprised and delighted as you re-introduce them to their favorite food—cheese!

Jean Paré

Each recipe has been analyzed using the most up-to-date version of the Canadian Nutrient File from Health Canada, which is based on the United States Department of Agriculture (USDA) Nutrient Data Base. If more that one ingredient is listed (such as "hard margarine or butter"), then the first ingredient is used in the analysis. Where an ingredient reads "sprinkle", "optional", or "for garnish", it is not included as part of the nutrition information.

Margaret Ng, B.Sc. (Hon), M.A.
Registered Dietitian

About Cheese

NUTRITION IN CHEESE

Cheese is usually made with cow's milk and contains protein, calcium, vitamins (vitamin A in particular) and minerals (such as phosphorus). Cheese is also lower in lactose (milk sugars)—the harder the cheese the less lactose it contains.

Light versus regular cheese: Lower-fat (also called light) cheese contains 25% less butterfat than regular cheese. It also tends to be higher in moisture content, more rubbery in texture, and less flavorful. Harder cheeses seem to convert better into the lower-fat format than softer cheeses, retaining more of their original texture and taste.

Bump up flavor with a sharper version of the lower-fat products if preferred. Some lower-fat cheeses or cream cheeses may not be suitable for baking or will produce less-than-desirable results. The higher moisture content may cause a runnier, less set product or a drier, crustier topping. Check labels for specific information.

SHOPPING FOR CHEESE

When buying cheese, consider the following:

- Buy in quantities of 1 lb. (454 g) or less. Sliced or shredded cheese has a shorter storage life so purchase these convenient products only when you have a specific use for them.
- Fresh cheese should have a matte appearance, without any "sweating" or cracking. Soft cheese should be evenly soft and spongy from center to edge. Firm cheese should have a bit of spring in the feel. The surface of blue cheese should be bright and colorful and the interior creamy, not dry.
- Check packaging to be sure it is airtight and undamaged.
- Always note the "best before" date to determine freshness.

STORING CHEESE

Store and chill all cheese in airtight containers or wrapped in plastic or foil. Stronger cheese should be wrapped, placed in a container and set apart from other foods. Store cheese in blocks no larger than 1 lb. (454 g).

Storage methods vary depending on types of cheese (see *Cheese Substitution Chart*, page 9). Hard cheeses refrigerate and freeze better than soft cheeses. Fresh cheeses do not freeze well so must be used before expiry date. Store brined cheese in its brine or in lightly salted water.

Firm and hard cheeses can be frozen for up to 6 months. Semi-soft cheeses are also freezer-friendly, but their texture may turn crumbly. When thawed, crumble into salads or use for melting. For best freezing results, never put room temperature cheese, including grated cheese, directly into freezer—always chill first.

Mold in cheese is either desirable, as in blue-veined cheeses, or undesirable, when found as fuzzy white or green spots on outside of cheese. Keep blue cheeses wrapped well and separate from other foods to avoid spore transfer.

COOKING WITH CHEESE

- The secret to cooking successfully with cheese is to keep the heat under the saucepan or fondue pot low. At about 150°F (65°C) cheese can begin to separate and, if cooked too long, turn stringy in texture. For best results, grate, chop or shred cheese first.
- 1/4 cup (60 mL) grated cheese = 1 oz. (28 g)*

For greater amounts, simply multiply the above base numbers.

- Harder cheese melts better than softer cheese and some cheese, like blue cheese, actually intensifies in flavor when heated.
- If using light cheese as a topping in a casserole, add cheese in the last 10 minutes or so of baking time, or cover with crumbs to keep the cheese from turning tough while baking.
- As you mix and heat ingredients for a sauce, add cheese last. Stir over low heat until cheese is melted.

SERVING CHEESE

- Serve cheese at room temperature. The exception is fresh cheese, such as cream cheese and cottage cheese, that should be served chilled.
- Avoid cutting cheese beforehand—instead serve on a wooden or marble board with a knife, and offer a separate knife for each kind of cheese to keep flavors apart.
- Cover cheese platter with plastic wrap or damp cloth before serving to avoid drying.
- Separate strong cheese from mild cheese.

Cheese Substitution Chart

Cheese Name	Flavor	Texture
Appenzeller Swiss, Kasseri, Parmesan, Romano, Roquefort, Sharp Cheddar	Strong	Hard
Blue, Blue Shropshire, Gorgonzola, Stilton	Strong	Soft
Brie, Camembert, Chèvre, Feta	Medium	Soft
Asiago, Gruyère, Kefalotyri, Medium Cheddar, Swiss	Medium	Firm
Gouda	Medium	Semi-soft
Colby, Longhorn, Mild Cheddar, Provolone, Samsoe	Mild	Firm
Halloumi, Havarti, Monterey Jack, Mozzarella, Muenster, Oka	Mild	Semi-soft
Cottage, Cream, Greek Myzithra, Quark, Ricotta		Fresh

Glossary of Cheese

This list describes many of the cheeses used in the recipes in this book.

Appenzeller Swiss (A-pent-seller): Pale interior and a washed, burnt-orange rind; familiar Swiss "eyes"; mild to nutty taste.

Asiago (ah-SYAH-goh): Pale yellow with tiny holes; may be coated with paraffin; mild to nutty flavor that becomes semi-sharp with age.

Blue: Soft and crumbly with characteristic blue veins; mild to tangy flavor that becomes peppery with age.

Blue Shropshire (SHRAHP-shur): English blue cheese that features royal blue veins in an orange interior with a rugged rind; strong, rich flavor.

Brie (BREE): White, soft interior with edible, dusty, white rind; classic buttery flavor.

Camembert (KAM-uhm-behr): Similar to Brie in looks but with firmer texture; milder flavor that develops a "tang" as it ripens.

Cheddar: Ivory or orange in color; texture grows firmer over time; flavors range from mild (aged 3 months) to extra sharp (aged 7 years).

Chèvre (SHEHV-ruh): French for goat cheese; comes in variety of textures and tastes.

Colby: Firm texture; mild flavor that grows stronger with age; milder version of Cheddar but with small "eyes."

Cottage: Fresh, small, white curds in milky liquid; mild flavor; also comes in dry curd form.

Cream: Smooth texture; hint of sharp taste; available in lower-fat and spreadable varieties.

Feta (FEHT-uh): Crumbly, fresh, white cheese with salty, pickled flavor; comes packaged in brine; may be made from cow's, goat's or ewe's milk; melts well.

Gorgonzola (gohr-gehn-ZOH-la): Italian cheese that has blue-green veins; goes from creamy to crumbly in texture as it ages; strong, robust, spicy taste.

Gouda (GOO-dah): Usually covered by red or yellow wax; nut-like flavor that grows with age. Flavored versions are available, identified by different wax colors; smoked variety is also available.

Greek Myzithra (or Mitzithra) (mih-ZEE-thra): Whey cheese with crumbly texture and mild, light taste; can come mixed with cream or milk or salted and dried to use as a grating cheese.

Gruyère (groo-YEHR): Smooth, firm texture and small "eyes"; buttery-tasting, medium-flavored; melts nicely.

Halloumi (huh-LOO-mee): Semi-soft texture more dense than mozzarella; mild, milky taste.

Havarti (hah-VAHR-tee): Light to yellow, with small, irregular "eyes"; taste is mild but tangy; flavored versions are available.

Kasseri (kuh-SEHR-ee): Hard Greek cheese made from sheep's milk and sometimes combined with goat's milk; sharp, salty and aromatic flavor.

Kefalotyri (keh-fuh-la-TEE-ree): Greek cheese made from sheep's milk; can vary in texture and taste by region, but generally firm and light colored with irregular holes; mild to medium flavor with slight tang.

Longhorn: Golden yellow cheese with firm crumbly texture; mild, Cheddar-like flavor.

Mascarpone (mas-car-POH-nay): Velvety soft fresh cream cheese; slightly acidic flavor; made from cow's milk; sold in tubs.

Monterey Jack: Ivory with tiny cracks in body; mild taste is underscored by nutty taste and may become more pronounced as it ages. A jalapeño-flavored version is also available.

Mozzarella (moht-sah-REHL-lah): Semi-soft, stringy, white-colored with a mild, delicate, milky taste; melts nicely.

Muenster (MUHN-stuhr): Mild in taste, with an edible orange rind; flavors mellow with age; not to be mistaken with French Muenster which has a much different taste.

Oka (OH-kah): Edible yellowish to reddish rind with a semi-hard center; nutty taste that ranges from mild to medium as it ages.

Parmesan (PAHR-muh-zahn): Hard and granular; full-bodied taste grows with age; grates well.

Provolone (proh-voh-LOH-nee): Golden; packaged in round, pear or tube shapes; hung in netting to age; has mild, slightly tart and salty flavor that develops with age.

Quark: Soft, fresh and white; light, lemon-fresh taste; smooth, creamy texture.

Ricotta (rih-KAHT-tuh): Resembles cottage cheese but more granular in texture; made from whey, not curd; taste is mild and semisweet.

Romano (roh-MAH-noh): Cream-colored, granular cheese with firm rind; grating cheese similar to Parmesan; strong, rich, robust taste.

Roquefort (ROHK-fuhrt): Famous French blue cheese; unique flavors derived from sheep's milk and an aging process in limestone caves; texture is smooth and firm, with a strong, but subtle flavor.

Samsoe: Firm, creamy white Danish cheese with holes; mild, nutty flavor that develops with age.

Stilton: One of Britain's most famous blue cheeses; sharp, nutty flavor that strengthens with age; creamy and crumbly, blue-veined interior.

Swiss: Firm, pale, smooth cheese with distinctive "eyes" and nutty flavor; available in a number of varieties.

Cheese Sticks

Using sea salt produces quite a salty
finished product that makes a great substitute for pretzels.

All-purpose flour	1 2/3 cups	400 mL
Baking powder	1/2 tsp.	2 mL
Dried whole oregano	1/4 tsp.	1 mL
Dried sweet basil	1/4 tsp.	1 mL
Parsley flakes	1/4 tsp.	1 mL
Dried thyme	1/4 tsp.	1 mL
Cayenne pepper	1/16 tsp.	0.5 mL
Butter (not margarine), chilled and cut into chunks	1/2 cup	125 mL
Grated Blue Shropshire cheese, chilled and packed (about 6 oz., 170 g)	1 1/2 cups	375 mL
Large egg	1	1
Half-and-half cream (or homogenized milk)	1 tbsp.	15 mL
Coarse sea salt (optional)	1 tbsp.	15 mL

Process first 7 ingredients in food processor for a few seconds until just mixed.

Add butter and cheese. Pulse with on/off motion several times until mixture resembles coarse crumbs.

Fork-beat egg and cream together in small cup. With motor running, slowly add egg mixture through feed chute until dough forms a ball and pulls away from sides of bowl. Divide dough into 2 equal portions. Shape each portion into a ball. Flatten into 2 discs. Cover in plastic wrap. Chill for 1 hour. Turn out onto lightly floured surface. Roll out 1 disc into 8 inch (20 cm) square. Cut in half. Cut each half into 16 sticks, using pizza cutter and ruler for nice straight sticks. Repeat with remaining disc.

Sprinkle sea salt over top. Arrange cheese sticks, salt side up, in single layer on greased baking sheets. Bake in 400°F (205°C) oven for about 10 minutes until golden and crisp. Cool on baking sheets. Makes 64 cheese sticks.

1 cheese stick: 39 Calories; 2.6 g Total Fat; 66 mg Sodium; 1 g Protein; 3 g Carbohydrate; trace Dietary Fiber

Pictured on page 17.

Variation: Omit Blue Shropshire cheese. Use same amount of Gorgonzola, Stilton or blue cheese.

Curried Mushroom And Feta Tarts

Small tarts with great curry and mushroom flavor.

Hard margarine (or butter)	1 tbsp.	15 mL
Curry paste	1/2 tsp.	2 mL
Finely chopped onion	1 tbsp.	15 mL
Sliced fresh mushrooms	1 1/2 cups	375 mL
Garlic clove, minced (or 1/8 tsp., 0.5 mL, powder), optional	1/2	1/2
Seasoned salt	1/4 tsp.	1 mL
Dried thyme	1/4 tsp.	1 mL
Pepper, sprinkle		
Finely crumbled feta cheese (about 2 1/2 oz., 70 g)	1/2 cup	125 mL
Cream Cheese Pastry, page 69 (1/2 recipe), or 24 unbaked mini-tart shells		
Large egg	1	1
Homogenized milk (or half-and-half cream)	1/4 cup	60 mL

Melt margarine and curry paste in frying pan. Add onion, mushrooms and garlic. Sauté until liquid from mushrooms has evaporated and mushrooms are golden.

Add seasoned salt, thyme and pepper. Stir. Cool.

Stir in cheese.

Line 24 mini-tart shells with pastry. Fill each with 1 1/2 tsp. (7 mL) mushroom mixture.

Fork-beat egg and milk together in small bowl. Divide evenly over mushroom mixture to fill shells about 2/3 full. Bake in 400°F (205°C) oven for about 12 minutes until golden. Makes 24 tarts.

1 tart: 52 Calories; 3.6 g Total Fat; 101 mg Sodium; 1 g Protein; 4 g Carbohydrate; trace Dietary Fiber

Pictured on page 17.

Feta-Stuffed Peppers

The creamy filling is piled onto slightly browned peppers.

Medium peppers (your choice of colors), cut into about 2 inch (5 cm) pieces	3	3
Boiling water, to cover		
Crumbled feta cheese	1 cup	250 mL
Chopped fresh oregano leaves (or 3/4 tsp., 4 mL, dried)	1 tbsp.	15 mL
Chopped fresh parsley (or 3/4 tsp., 4 mL, flakes)	1 tbsp.	15 mL
Balsamic vinegar	2 tsp.	10 mL
Olive (or cooking) oil	2 tsp.	10 mL
Finely chopped ripe olives	2 tbsp.	30 mL
Finely chopped garlic (or powder, sprinkle), optional	1/4 tsp.	1 mL
Block of cream cheese (4 oz., 125 g, size)	1/4	1/4

Cook peppers in boiling water for 2 minutes. Immediately plunge into ice water. Blot dry with paper towel.

Combine remaining 8 ingredients in small bowl. Spoon about 2 tsp. (10 mL) onto each pepper piece. Arrange stuffed pepper pieces in single layer on ungreased baking sheet. Bake in 350°F (175°C) oven for 15 to 20 minutes until peppers are tender-crisp. Makes about 24 pieces.

1 piece: 37 Calories; 3 g Total Fat; 85 mg Sodium; 1 g Protein; 2 g Carbohydrate; trace Dietary Fiber

Pictured on front cover.

Paré Pointer

Bring us a crocodile sandwich right away and make it snappy.

Appetizers

Herbed Feta Spread

This spread has a wonderful Greek flavor. Spoon onto crackers or toasted baguette slices. This recipe is best with fresh basil and oregano leaves.

Olive (or cooking) oil	3 tbsp.	50 mL
Garlic cloves, minced (or 1/4 - 1/2 tsp., 1 - 2 mL, powder)	1 - 2	1 - 2
Crumbled feta cheese (about 10 oz., 285 g)	2 cups	500 mL
Sliced green onion	1/4 cup	60 mL
Paprika	1/2 tsp.	2 mL
Fresh sweet basil leaves	8 - 10	8 - 10
Fresh oregano leaves	8 - 10	8 - 10
Rosemary sprig	1	1
Pine nuts, toasted (see Tip, below) and chopped (optional)	1 tbsp.	15 mL

Combine olive oil and garlic in small cup. Drizzle about 1/2 into small glass pie plate. Brush on bottom and up sides.

Sprinkle cheese over olive oil mixture. Sprinkle green onion and paprika over top. Drizzle with remaining olive oil mixture.

Cover with basil and oregano leaves. Lay rosemary sprig on top. Cover tightly with foil. Bake in 400°F (205°C) oven for 25 to 30 minutes until hot. Remove and discard basil, oregano and rosemary.

Sprinkle pine nuts over top. Serve warm. Makes about 2 cups (500 mL).

1/2 cup (125 mL): 289 Calories; 26 g Total Fat; 823 mg Sodium; 11 g Protein; 4 g Carbohydrate; trace Dietary Fiber

Pictured on page 18.

 To toast almonds, pine nuts and sesame seeds, place in single layer in ungreased shallow pan. Bake in 350°F (175°C) oven for 5 to 10 minutes, stirring or shaking often, until desired doneness.

Pastry Twists

These attractive pastries are great to serve as an appetizer and as a dipper for hot cheese dip, salsa or chili. Very easy to make.

Package of frozen puff pastry (14 oz., 397 g), thawed according to package directions	1/2	1/2
Milk	2 tbsp.	30 mL
Grated Romano (or extra sharp Cheddar or Parmesan) cheese (about 1 1/3 oz., 37 g)	1/3 cup	75 mL
No-salt seasoning (see Note), sprinkle (optional)		

Roll out pastry on lightly floured surface to 9 × 12 inch (22 × 30 cm) rectangle. Brush with 1/2 of milk. Sprinkle with 1/2 of cheese and seasoning. Roll out slightly just to press cheese into pastry. Turn over. Brush with remaining milk. Sprinkle with remaining cheese and seasoning. Roll out slightly just to press cheese into pastry. Cut in half crosswise, making two 6 × 9 inch (15 × 22 cm) rectangles. Cut each rectangle crosswise, into 1 inch (2.5 cm) strips. Twist each strip 2 to 3 times. Arrange 3 inches (7.5 cm) apart on greased baking sheet. Bake in 375°F (190°C) oven for about 12 minutes until golden. Remove to wire rack to cool. Makes 18 twists.

1 twist: 69 Calories; 4.7 g Total Fat; 52 mg Sodium; 1 g Protein; 5 g Carbohydrate; 0 g Dietary Fiber

Pictured on page 17.

Note: Use your choice of no-salt seasoning such as Italian, Mediterranean, Greek, roasted garlic or herb.

1. Pastry Twists, above
2. Cheese Sticks, page 12
3. Wee Sandwich Balls, page 21
4. Curried Mushroom And Feta Tarts, page 13
5. Quick Quiches, page 20
6. Fried Cheese, page 23
7. Appetizer Corn Wedges, page 22

Props Courtesy Of: Linens 'N Things

Oriental Cheese Spread

Block of cream cheese marinated in soy sauce, ginger and onion.
Very yummy. Serve with a variety of crackers.

Soy sauce	1/2 cup	125 mL
Icing (confectioner's) sugar	1/4 cup	60 mL
Finely chopped green onion	3 tbsp.	50 mL
Finely chopped garlic (optional)	1/2 tsp.	2 mL
Minced crystallized ginger	1 1/2 tbsp.	25 mL
Dried crushed chilies	1 tsp.	5 mL
Block of cream cheese	8 oz.	250 g
Sesame seeds, toasted (see Tip, page 15)	3 tbsp.	50 mL

Combine first 6 ingredients in shallow bowl. Stir until sugar is dissolved. Pour into resealable plastic bag. Makes 3/4 cup (175 mL) marinade.

Add cream cheese. Seal bag. Turn to coat. Marinate in refrigerator for 3 days, turning occasionally.

Remove cream cheese. Press into sesame seeds until completely coated. Place on serving plate. Sprinkle remaining sesame seeds over top. Serves 8 to 10.

1 serving: 162 Calories; 12.7 g Total Fat; 1186 mg Sodium; 5 g Protein; 8 g Carbohydrate; 1 g Dietary Fiber

Pictured on page 18.

Variation: Omit plain sesame seeds. Use black sesame seeds.

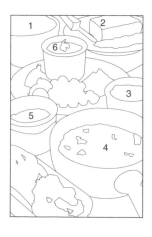

1. Artichoke Tomato Chèvre Spread, page 20
2. Oriental Cheese Spread, above
3. Blue Cheese Dip, page 24
4. Herbed Feta Spread, page 15
5. Skinny Dipping, page 25
6. Key Lime Fruit Dip, page 24

Artichoke Tomato Chèvre Spread

A marinated dish to serve on baguette slices, crackers or focaccia bread.

Olive (or cooking) oil	1/2 cup	125 mL
Garlic cloves, minced (or 3/4 tsp., 4 mL, powder)	3	3
Jar of marinated artichoke hearts, drained and chopped	6 oz.	170 mL
Medium roma (plum) tomatoes, seeded and diced (about 3/4 cup, 175 mL)	2	2
Finely chopped fresh sweet basil (or 1 1/2 tsp., 7 mL, dried)	2 tbsp.	30 mL
Crumbled Chèvre cheese (about 15 oz., 425 g)	3 cups	750 mL
Sliced ripe olives	1/3 cup	75 mL
Chopped pine nuts (optional), toasted (see Tip, page 15)	1 – 2 tbsp.	15 – 30 mL

Mix first 7 ingredients in medium bowl. Cover. Marinate in refrigerator for several hours or overnight.

To serve, bring to room temperature. Sprinkle pine nuts over top. Makes 3 1/3 cups (825 mL).

2 tbsp. (30 mL): 101 Calories; 9.1 g Total Fat; 105 mg Sodium; 4 g Protein; 1 g Carbohydrate; trace Dietary Fiber

Pictured on page 18.

Quick Quiches

The distinct flavors of Gruyère cheese and onion are evident.

Large eggs	2	2
Finely chopped onion	1/2 cup	125 mL
Skim evaporated milk (or milk)	1/2 cup	125 mL
Salt	1/4 tsp.	1 mL
Pepper	1/16 tsp.	0.5 mL
Ground nutmeg, just a pinch		

(continued on next page)

Appetizers

Unbaked mini-tart shells	24	24
Grated Gruyère cheese (about 4 oz., 113 g)	1 cup	250 mL
Sliced pimiento, for garnish	1/3 cup	75 mL

Put first 6 ingredients into blender. Process until smooth.

Place tart shells on baking sheet. Divide cheese evenly among tart shells. Divide and pour egg mixture over cheese.

Garnish with pimiento. Bake in 350°F (175°C) oven for about 20 minutes until set. Makes 24 quiches.

1 quiche: 64 Calories; 4 g Total Fat; 93 mg Sodium; 3 g Protein; 4 g Carbohydrate; trace Dietary Fiber

Pictured on page 17.

Wee Sandwich Balls

These one-bite appetizers will appeal to your guests.

Block of cream cheese, softened	4 oz.	125 g
Grated Monterey Jack cheese (about 3 oz., 85 g)	3/4 cup	175 mL
Grated medium Cheddar cheese (about 3 oz., 85 g)	3/4 cup	175 mL
Finely chopped ham, blotted dry	2/3 cup	150 mL
Finely chopped dill pickle, blotted dry	3 tbsp.	50 mL
Fresh whole wheat bread crumbs (about 2 slices)	2/3 cup	150 mL
Finely chopped fresh parsley (or 3/4 tsp., 4 mL, flakes)	1 tbsp.	15 mL
Seasoned salt	1/4 tsp.	1 mL

Cream all 3 cheeses together in medium bowl. Add ham and dill pickle. Stir. Shape into small balls, using about 1 tbsp. (15 mL) for each.

Combine bread crumbs, parsley and seasoned salt in small bowl. Roll cheese balls in crumb mixture to coat completely. Makes about 26 sandwich balls.

1 sandwich ball: 56 Calories; 4.4 g Total Fat; 141 mg Sodium; 3 g Protein; 1 g Carbohydrate; trace Dietary Fiber

Pictured on page 17.

Appetizer Corn Wedges

Yellow wedges with green and yellow bits throughout.
Cheese both in and on each yummy piece. These are good hot or cold.

Can of condensed chicken broth	10 oz.	284 mL
Water	1 1/2 cups	375 mL
Roasted garlic and pepper seasoning mix (or other herb seasoning mix)	1 tbsp.	15 mL
Yellow cornmeal	3/4 cup	175 mL
Cooked corn kernels (fresh or frozen), chopped	1 cup	250 mL
Parsley flakes	2 tsp.	10 mL
Jalapeño pepper, seeded and finely diced (see Note)	1	1
Grated Romano cheese (about 3/4 oz., 21 g)	1/4 cup	60 mL
Olive (or cooking) oil	1 tbsp.	15 mL
Grated Monterey Jack With Jalapeño cheese (about 3 oz., 85 g)	1 cup	250 mL

Combine broth, water and seasoning mix in large non-stick frying pan. Bring to a boil. Reduce heat to medium-low. Slowly stir in cornmeal. Simmer for about 10 minutes, stirring frequently, until very thick and stiff.

Stir in corn, parsley flakes and jalapeño pepper. Cook on low for about 3 minutes until very thick and leaves side of saucepan. Remove from heat.

Add Romano cheese. Stir until melted.

Brush bottom and sides of 9 × 9 inch (22 × 22 cm) pan with 1/2 of olive oil. Spread cornmeal mixture evenly in pan. Brush surface with remaining olive oil. Chill for at least 6 hours or overnight. Turn out onto cutting surface. Cut with wet knife into 6 rows across and 3 rows down. Cut each piece in half diagonally to make a total of 36 wedges. Arrange, not touching, on greased baking sheet. Broil on top rack for 3 minutes. Turn over. Broil until edges are golden.

Move wedges close together. Sprinkle with Monterey Jack cheese. Broil for about 1 minute until cheese is melted. Makes 36 wedges.

1 wedge: 38 Calories; 1.8 g Total Fat; 80 mg Sodium; 2 g Protein; 4 g Carbohydrate; trace Dietary Fiber

Pictured on page 17.

Note: Wear gloves when chopping jalapeño peppers and avoid touching your eyes.

Fried Cheese

This popular appetizer is always enjoyed by all.
Change flavor by using different kinds of seasoning mixes.

Variety of cheeses (such as mozzarella, Halloumi, Gouda, Smoked Gouda, Monterey Jack With Jalapeño, Brie, Camembert)	1 lb.	454 g
Milk	1/2 cup	125 mL
All-purpose flour	1/3 cup	75 mL
No-salt seasoning (see Note), optional	2 tsp.	10 mL
Paprika	1 tsp.	5 mL
Pepper, sprinkle		
Large eggs	3	3
Water	1/4 cup	60 mL
Fine dry bread crumbs	1 1/2 cups	375 mL
Cooking oil, for deep-frying		

Cut cheese into sticks 1/2 to 3/4 inch (1.2 to 2 cm) wide and 3 inches (7.5 cm) long. If using small round cheese, such as Brie or Camembert, cut into 6 to 8 wedges.

Place milk in small shallow bowl.

Mix flour, seasoning, paprika and pepper in shallow dish.

Fork-beat eggs and water together in small bowl.

Place bread crumbs in separate shallow dish. Dip cheese into milk. Press into flour mixture to coat completely. Dip into egg mixture. Press into bread crumbs to coat completely. Dip into egg mixture a second time. Press into bread crumbs again to coat completely. Place on waxed paper-lined baking sheet. Chill for 1 to 2 hours until dry.

Deep-fry in hot (375°F, 190°C) cooking oil for 3 to 4 minutes, gently turning a few times, until golden. Remove with slotted spoon to paper towels to drain. Serve warm. Makes about 18 sticks.

1 stick: 158 Calories; 9.5 g Total Fat; 247 mg Sodium; 8 g Protein; 10 g Carbohydrate; 1 g Dietary Fiber

Pictured on page 17.

Note: Use your choice of no-salt seasoning such as Italian, Mediterranean, Greek, roasted garlic or herb.

Key Lime Fruit Dip

Tangy yet a bit sweet and just a hint of coconut.

Block of cream cheese, softened	4 oz.	125 g
Key lime (or lime or lemon) juice (see Note)	2 tbsp.	30 mL
White corn syrup	2 tbsp.	30 mL
Whipping cream	1/2 cup	125 mL
Coconut powder	1/4 cup	60 mL

Finely grated lime peel, for garnish

Beat cream cheese, lime juice and corn syrup together in medium bowl until fluffy and smooth.

Beat whipping cream and coconut powder together, using same beaters, in small bowl on low until blended. Beat on high until stiff peaks form. Fold into cream cheese mixture. Cover. Chill for 1 hour.

Garnish with lime peel. Makes 1 3/4 cups (425 mL).

2 tbsp. (30 mL): 75 Calories; 6.6 g Total Fat; 33 mg Sodium; 1 g Protein; 3 g Carbohydrate; trace Dietary Fiber

Pictured on page 18.

Note: Key lime juice can often be found in the juice aisle of larger grocery stores or in specialty food stores.

Blue Cheese Dip

The best dip ever! Try with wings, veggies, hamburgers, sandwiches or even potato chips.

Mayonnaise	1/2 cup	125 mL
Sour cream	1/4 cup	60 mL
Crumbled blue cheese	2 tbsp.	30 mL
Dried chives	2 tsp.	10 mL
Minced onion flakes, crushed	2 tsp.	10 mL

Mix all 5 ingredients in small bowl. Chill for at least 1 hour to blend flavors. Makes about 1 cup (250 mL).

2 tbsp. (30 mL): 127 Calories; 12.9 g Total Fat; 105 mg Sodium; 1 g Protein; 2 g Carbohydrate; trace Dietary Fiber

Pictured on page 18.

Skinny Dipping

This dip uses cottage cheese for a lower-in-fat treat. Fresh dill flavor.

Creamed cottage cheese	1 cup	250 mL
Lemon juice	1 1/2 tsp.	7 mL
Chopped fresh dill (or 1 1/2 tsp., 7 mL, dill weed)	2 tbsp.	30 mL
Chopped chives	1 tsp.	5 mL
Seasoned salt	1/8 tsp.	0.5 mL

Put all 5 ingredients into blender. Process until smooth. Makes about 1 cup (250 mL).

2 tbsp. (30 mL): 28 Calories; 1.2 g Total Fat; 126 mg Sodium; 3 g Protein; 1 g Carbohydrate; 0 g Dietary Fiber

Pictured on page 18.

Ranchers' Dip

A nippy dip. Serve warm with tortilla chips or any other cracker.

Jar of jalapeño bean dip	9 oz.	255 g
Grated Monterey Jack cheese (about 4 oz., 113 g)	1 cup	250 mL
Light sour cream	1 cup	250 mL
Block of light cream cheese, softened	4 oz.	125 g
Chopped green onion	1/4 cup	60 mL
Cayenne pepper	1/8 tsp.	0.5 mL
Onion powder	1/4 tsp.	1 mL
Grated Monterey Jack cheese (about 4 oz., 113 g)	1 cup	250 mL
Grated sharp Cheddar cheese (about 4 oz., 113 g)	1 cup	250 mL
Chili powder	1 tsp.	5 mL

Put first 7 ingredients into large bowl. Mash together with fork. Spread in 9 inch (22 cm) pie plate.

Sprinkle Monterey Jack cheese, Cheddar cheese and chili powder over top. Heat in 350°F (175°C) oven for about 20 minutes until heated through and cheese is melted. Serves 8 to 10.

1 serving: 264 Calories; 19.6 g Total Fat; 510 mg Sodium; 15 g Protein; 7 g Carbohydrate; 2 g Dietary Fiber

Flaxseed Cheese Sticks

Two kinds of cheese flavor these big bread sticks.
The flaxseed gives a bit of interest.

Warm water	2/3 cup	150 mL
Warm milk	2/3 cup	150 mL
Hard margarine (or butter)	2 tbsp.	30 mL
Liquid honey	1 tbsp.	15 mL
Salt	1 1/2 tsp.	7 mL
All-purpose flour	2 cups	500 mL
Instant yeast (or 1/4 oz., 8 g, envelope)	2 1/4 tsp.	11 mL
Whole wheat flour	1 cup	250 mL
Grated Parmesan cheese	1/4 cup	60 mL
Flaxseed	4 tsp.	20 mL
All-purpose flour, approximately	2/3 cup	150 mL
Grated medium Cheddar cheese (about 8 oz., 225 g)	2 cups	500 mL

Heat and stir first 5 ingredients in small saucepan until margarine is melted. Pour into large bowl. Cool slightly. Mixture should still be very warm.

Combine first amount of all-purpose flour and yeast in small bowl. Stir into milk mixture until flour is just moistened. Mix with spoon for 1 to 2 minutes to dissolve yeast.

Work in whole wheat flour, Parmesan cheese and flaxseed until soft dough forms. Turn out onto lightly floured surface. Knead for about 5 minutes, adding enough of second amount of all-purpose flour until dough is no longer sticky. Divide dough into 12 equal portions. Form each portion into oblong shape. Arrange cheese sticks, about 2 inches (5 cm) apart, on greased baking sheet. Cover with tea towel. Let stand in oven with light on and door closed for about 1 hour until doubled in size.

Divide and sprinkle Cheddar cheese over cheese sticks. Bake on center rack in 350°F (175°C) oven for 18 to 20 minutes until golden. Remove to wire rack to cool. Makes 12 cheese sticks.

1 cheese stick: 268 Calories; 10.2 g Total Fat; 493 mg Sodium; 11 g Protein; 33 g Carbohydrate; 3 g Dietary Fiber

Pictured on page 126.

Zucchini Cheese Pull-Aparts

Wonderful rosemary and Asiago cheese flavors. Pretty and moist buns.

Grated zucchini	2 cups	500 mL
Salt	1 tbsp.	15 mL
Warm water	1 cup	250 mL
Granulated sugar	2 tsp.	10 mL
Active dry yeast	1 1/2 tbsp.	25 mL
All-purpose flour	4 cups	1 L
Grated Asiago cheese (about 3 oz., 85 g)	3/4 cup	175 mL
Olive (or cooking) oil	2 tbsp.	30 mL
Dried rosemary	2 tsp.	10 mL
Salt	1/2 tsp.	2 mL
Warm water	1 cup	250 mL
All-purpose flour, approximately	2 cups	500 mL

Place zucchini in colander. Sprinkle with first amount of salt. Let drain for 30 minutes. Rinse thoroughly. Pat dry.

Stir first amount of water and sugar in small bowl until sugar is dissolved. Sprinkle yeast over top. Let stand for 10 minutes. Stir to dissolve yeast. Transfer to large bowl.

Add next 5 ingredients. Gradually mix in second amount of water until dough is very sticky. Turn out onto lightly floured surface.

Gently knead in zucchini and enough of second amount of flour until dough is smooth and elastic. Place in lightly greased bowl, turning once to grease top. Cover with tea towel. Let stand in oven with light on and door closed for about 1 1/2 hours until doubled in bulk. Punch dough down. Shape into 32 buns. Arrange, nearly touching, on 12 inch (30 cm) pizza pan or greased 10 x 15 inch (25 x 38 cm) jelly roll pan. Cover. Let stand in oven with light on and door closed for about 1 hour until doubled in size. Bake in 350°F (175°C) oven for 25 to 30 minutes until golden. Makes 32 pull-aparts.

1 pull-apart: 111 Calories; 1.8 g Total Fat; 50 mg Sodium; 3 g Protein; 20 g Carbohydrate; 1 g Dietary Fiber

Pictured on page 90.

Apple Cheese Loaf

Especially good when served lightly buttered or with a thin cheese slice.

Hard margarine (or butter), softened	1/2 cup	125 mL
Granulated sugar	3/4 cup	175 mL
Large eggs	2	2
Grated sharp Cheddar cheese (about 2 oz., 57 g)	1/2 cup	125 mL
Peeled and coarsely grated cooking apple (such as McIntosh)	1 cup	250 mL
All-purpose flour	2 1/2 cups	625 mL
Baking powder	2 tsp.	10 mL
Baking soda	1 tsp.	5 mL
Salt	1 tsp.	5 mL
Chopped walnuts (optional)	1/2 cup	125 mL

Cream margarine and sugar together in large bowl. Beat in eggs, 1 at a time, beating well after each addition.

Add cheese and apple. Stir.

Combine remaining 5 ingredients in medium bowl. Add to apple mixture. Stir until just moistened. Turn into greased 9 x 5 x 3 inch (22 x 12.5 x 7.5 cm) loaf pan. Bake in 350°F (175°C) oven for about 50 minutes until wooden pick inserted in center comes out clean. Let stand in pan for 10 minutes before turning out onto wire rack to cool. Cuts into 16 slices.

1 slice: 196 Calories; 8.1 g Total Fat; 377 mg Sodium; 4 g Protein; 27 g Carbohydrate; 1 g Dietary Fiber

Feta Dill Biscuits

These are so flaky and delicious with bursts of feta in every bite. Yummy with Broccoli Cheese Soup, page 145, and Cheddar Chicken Soup, page 148.

All-purpose flour	2 cups	500 mL
Baking powder	4 tsp.	20 mL
Granulated sugar	1 tsp.	5 mL
Salt	1/2 tsp.	2 mL
Chopped fresh dill (or 3/4 tsp., 4 mL, dill weed)	1 tbsp.	15 mL
Hard margarine (or butter)	6 tbsp.	100 mL

(continued on next page)

Crumbled feta cheese (about 5 oz., 140 g)	1 cup	250 mL
Milk	1/2 cup	125 mL
Water	1/4 cup	60 mL

Combine first 5 ingredients in large bowl. Cut in margarine until crumbly.

Add cheese. Stir. Add milk and water. Stir until dough forms a ball. Turn out onto lightly floured surface. Knead 6 to 8 times. Pat or roll out to 3/4 inch (2 cm) thickness. Cut with 2 inch (5 cm) round cutter. Arrange on ungreased baking sheet close together for moist edges or 1 inch (2.5 cm) apart for crisp edges. Bake in 425°F (220°C) oven for 12 to 15 minutes until risen and golden. Makes 22 biscuits.

1 biscuit: 95 Calories; 4.9 g Total Fat; 245 mg Sodium; 3 g Protein; 10 g Carbohydrate; trace Dietary Fiber

Pictured on page 144.

CHEDDAR DILL BISCUITS: Omit feta. Add same amount of grated sharp Cheddar cheese (about 5 oz., 140 g).

Savory Cheese Bread

Mild oregano flavor. Delicious with Veggie Cheese Soup, page 146.

All-purpose flour	2 1/2 cups	625 mL
Baking powder	4 tsp.	20 mL
Granulated sugar	1 tbsp.	15 mL
Onion salt	1/2 tsp.	2 mL
Dry mustard	1/4 tsp.	1 mL
Garlic salt	1/4 tsp.	1 mL
Dried whole oregano	1/4 tsp.	1 mL
Grated sharp Cheddar cheese (about 5 oz., 140 g)	1 1/4 cups	300 mL
Large egg, fork-beaten	1	1
Cooking oil	2 tbsp.	30 mL
Milk	1 1/4 cups	300 mL

Combine first 8 ingredients in large bowl. Make a well in center.

Pour egg, cooking oil and milk into well. Stir until just moistened. Turn into greased 9 x 5 x 3 inch (22 x 12.5 x 7.5 cm) loaf pan. Bake in 350°F (175°C) oven for about 40 minutes until wooden pick inserted in center comes out clean. Turn out onto wire rack to cool. Cuts into 16 slices.

1 slice: 145 Calories; 5.6 g Total Fat; 221 mg Sodium; 6 g Protein; 18 g Carbohydrate; 1 g Dietary Fiber

Pictured on page 144.

Blue Cheese Pistachio Bread

Heavy golden brown bread with strong blue cheese flavor and crunchy nuts.

All-purpose flour	3 cups	750 mL
Baking powder	4 tsp.	20 mL
Salt	1/2 tsp.	2 mL
Dried sweet basil	1 tsp.	5 mL
Crumbled blue cheese	1/2 cup	125 mL
Chopped shelled pistachios	3/4 cup	175 mL
Large eggs	2	2
Milk	1 1/4 cups	300 mL

Combine first 6 ingredients in large bowl.

Fork-beat eggs and milk together in small bowl. Add to flour mixture. Stir until just moistened. Turn into greased 9 x 5 x 3 inch (22 x 12.5 x 7.5 cm) loaf pan. Bake in 350°F (175°C) oven for about 50 minutes until wooden pick inserted in center comes out clean. Let stand in pan for 10 minutes before turning out onto wire rack to cool. Cuts into 16 slices.

1 slice: 161 Calories; 5.4 g Total Fat; 248 mg Sodium; 6 g Protein; 22 g Carbohydrate; 1 g Dietary Fiber

Pictured on front cover.

Mom's Cheese Biscuits

Great with Cheesy Spinach Soup, page 147, or Creamed Onion Soup, page 141.

All-purpose flour	2 cups	500 mL
Dry mustard	1 tbsp.	15 mL
Baking powder	1 tbsp.	15 mL
Salt	1/2 tsp.	2 mL
Pepper	1/4 tsp.	1 mL
Hard margarine (or butter)	1/3 cup	75 mL
Grated sharp Cheddar cheese (about 4 oz., 113 g)	1 cup	250 mL
Milk	1 cup	250 mL

(continued on next page)

Measure first 5 ingredients into medium bowl. Stir. Cut in margarine until crumbly.

Add cheese. Stir. Stir in milk until dough is moistened and sticky. Drop by rounded tablespoonfuls onto greased baking sheet. Bake in 450°F (230°C) oven for about 15 minutes until golden. Makes 16 biscuits.

1 biscuit: 137 Calories; 7 g Total Fat; 245 mg Sodium; 4 g Protein; 14 g Carbohydrate; 1 g Dietary Fiber

Crabby Cheese Bites

A different yet tasty snack that will keep your friends dropping by for more.

Grated medium Cheddar cheese (about 3/4 lb., 340 g)	3 cups	750 mL
Hard margarine (or butter), softened	1/4 cup	60 mL
Can of crabmeat, drained, cartilage removed, flaked	4 1/4 oz.	120 g
Fresh asparagus spears, cooked	24	24
Hamburger buns (or English muffins), split (buttered, optional)	6	6

Mix cheese and margarine in medium bowl until well combined.

Add crab. Stir well.

Place 2 asparagus spears on each bun half. Spears can be cut to fit. Top each with 1/4 cup (60 mL) cheese mixture. Arrange in single layer on ungreased baking sheet. Bake in 350°F (175°C) oven for 10 to 12 minutes until hot and bubbly. Makes 12 cheese bites.

1 cheese bite: 232 Calories; 15.2 g Total Fat; 427 mg Sodium; 12 g Protein; 13 g Carbohydrate; trace Dietary Fiber

 To prevent cheese from absorbing food odors, do not store with other strong-smelling foods such as spicy sandwich meats. Store in airtight container or wrap tightly. As cheese breathes, it will absorb the other odors which may change the taste.

Breakfast Pizza

The addition of bran to the crust makes this a natural for breakfast.

BRAN PIZZA CRUST

All-purpose flour	1 1/2 cups	375 mL
Natural wheat bran	2/3 cup	150 mL
Granulated sugar	1 tsp.	5 mL
Salt	1/4 tsp.	1 mL
Instant yeast	1 1/4 tsp.	6 mL
Warm water	2/3 cup	150 mL
Fancy (mild) molasses	2 tbsp.	30 mL
Cooking oil	2 tbsp.	30 mL

TOPPING

Bacon slices, diced	8	8
Chopped onion	1/2 cup	125 mL
Large eggs, fork-beaten	6	6
Water	3 tbsp.	50 mL
Salt	1/2 tsp.	2 mL
Pepper, sprinkle		
Ketchup	1/3 cup	75 mL
Frozen potato tots, thawed (add more if desired)	15	15
Grated part-skim mozzarella cheese (about 3 oz., 85 g)	3/4 cup	175 mL
Grated Dofino (or Havarti) cheese (about 3 oz., 85 g)	3/4 cup	175 mL

Bran Pizza Crust: Food Processor Method: Put first 5 ingredients into food processor fitted with dough blade.

With machine running, pour next 3 ingredients through feed chute. Process for 50 to 60 seconds. If dough seems too sticky add flour, 1/2 tsp. (2 mL) at a time, until dough is no longer sticky.

Hand Method: Measure first 5 ingredients into large bowl. Stir together well.

Add next 3 ingredients. Mix well until dough leaves sides of bowl. Turn out onto lightly floured surface. Knead for 5 to 8 minutes until smooth and elastic.

(continued on next page)

Brunch

To complete, place dough in greased bowl, turning once to grease top. Cover with tea towel. Let stand in oven with light on and door closed for about 1 hour until doubled in bulk. Punch dough down. Roll out and press into greased 12 inch (30 cm) pizza pan, forming rim around edge. Poke holes all over with fork. Bake on bottom rack in 425°F (220°C) oven for 10 minutes. Using paper towel to protect hands, press bumps down.

Topping: Sauté bacon and onion in frying pan until bacon is golden and onion is soft. Drain well.

Add eggs, water, salt and pepper. Heat and stir until egg is half cooked.

Spread ketchup over hot crust. Spoon egg mixture over top. Arrange potato tots over egg mixture.

Toss both cheeses together in small bowl. Sprinkle over potato tots. Bake for about 15 minutes until cheese is melted. Cuts into 8 wedges.

1 wedge: 354 Calories; 17.1 g Total Fat; 735 mg Sodium; 17 g Protein; 35 g Carbohydrate; 4 g Dietary Fiber

Bacon Cheese Strata

Beautiful golden brown with delightful taste. Serve with Parma Rosa Sauce, page 122, tomato sauce or fruit salad.

Day-old white bread slices, crusts removed	8	8
Grated medium Cheddar cheese (about 8 oz., 225 g)	2 cups	500 mL
Bacon slices, cooked crisp and crumbled	6	6
Large eggs	4	4
Milk	2 cups	500 mL
Worcestershire sauce	1 tsp.	5 mL
Salt	1/2 tsp.	2 mL
Pepper	1/8 tsp.	0.5 mL
Onion powder	1/4 tsp.	1 mL

Fit 1/2 of bread slices into bottom of greased 9 x 9 inch (22 x 22 cm) pan. Sprinkle with cheese and bacon. Fit remaining bread slices over top.

Beat remaining 6 ingredients together in medium bowl. Pour over bread slices. Cover. Chill for several hours or overnight. Bake, uncovered, in 350°F (175°C) oven for 40 to 50 minutes until golden. Cuts into 6 pieces.

1 piece: 364 Calories; 21.6 g Total Fat; 802 mg Sodium; 21 g Protein; 20 g Carbohydrate; 1 g Dietary Fiber

Brunch

Zucchini Potato Pancakes

A thin golden pancake with mild garlic and pepper taste. Serve with sour cream.

All-purpose flour	1/4 cup	60 mL
Baking powder	1/4 tsp.	1 mL
Grated Gouda cheese (about 6 oz., 170 g)	1 1/2 cups	375 mL
Large eggs, fork-beaten	3	3
Garlic salt	3/4 - 1 tsp.	4 - 5 mL
Pepper	1/4 tsp.	1 mL
Medium zucchini, with peel, coarsely grated (about 1 1/2 cups, 375 mL)	1	1
Sliced green onion	1/3 cup	75 mL
Medium baking potatoes, coarsely grated (about 1 1/2 cups, 375 mL)	2	2
Cooking oil, approximately	1 tsp.	5 mL

Combine first 9 ingredients, in order given, in large bowl.

Heat cooking oil in large frying pan on medium until hot. Drop about 1/4 cup (60 mL) batter into frying pan. Flatten as much as possible. Cook for 2 to 3 minutes per side until golden and crisp. Add more cooking oil as necessary to keep pancakes from sticking to pan and allowing edges to crisp. Makes 12 pancakes.

1 pancake: 114 Calories; 6.6 g Total Fat; 246 mg Sodium; 7 g Protein; 7 g Carbohydrate; 1 g Dietary Fiber

Pictured on page 35.

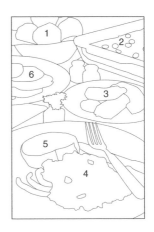

Bacon Herb Muffins

A good breakfast muffin. Airy texture, subtle flavors, lightly golden.

Bacon slices, cooked crisp and crumbled	4	4
Whole wheat flour	1 1/4 cups	300 mL
All-purpose flour	1 1/4 cups	300 mL
Baking powder	1 tbsp.	15 mL
Salt	1/4 tsp.	1 mL
Dried sweet basil (see Note)	1/2 tsp.	2 mL
Dried whole oregano (see Note)	1/2 tsp.	2 mL
Grated sharp Cheddar cheese (about 4 oz., 113 g)	1 cup	250 mL
Hard margarine (or butter), melted	1/2 cup	125 mL
Large eggs, fork-beaten	2	2
Buttermilk (or reconstituted from powder)	1 cup	250 mL
Liquid honey	1 tbsp.	15 mL

Combine first 7 ingredients in large bowl.

Add remaining 5 ingredients. Stir until just moistened. Fill greased muffin cups 3/4 full. Bake in 400°F (205°C) oven for 17 to 20 minutes until wooden pick inserted in center comes out clean. Let stand in pan for 5 minutes. Remove to wire rack to cool. Makes 12 muffins.

1 muffin: 247 Calories; 13.8 g Total Fat; 366 mg Sodium; 8 g Protein; 23 g Carbohydrate; 2 g Dietary Fiber

Pictured on page 35.

Note: If you are really fond of herbs, double the amounts of basil and oregano.

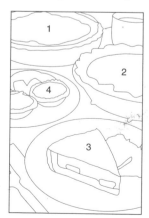

1. Chicken Quiche, page 49
2. Blue Onion Pie, page 48
3. Stuffing Crust Quiche, page 46
4. Mushroom Quiche, page 47

Props Courtesy Of: Pfaltzgraff Canada

Orange Cinnamon Blintzes

Moist crêpes with orange and cottage cheese filling.
Top with sour cream or jam for wonderful flavor.

CRÊPES

All-purpose flour	1 cup	250 mL
Brown sugar, packed	1 tbsp.	15 mL
Salt	1/4 tsp.	1 mL
Ground cinnamon	1/8 tsp.	0.5 mL
Large eggs	3	3
Egg white (large)	1	1
Milk	3/4 cup	175 mL
Prepared orange juice	1/2 cup	125 mL
Hard margarine (or butter), melted	3 tbsp.	50 mL

COTTAGE CHEESE FILLING

Dry curd cottage cheese	17 1/2 oz.	500 g
Egg yolk (large)	1	1
Freshly grated orange peel	2 tsp.	10 mL
Granulated sugar	2 tbsp.	30 mL
Salt	1/4 tsp.	1 mL
Ground cinnamon	1/8 tsp.	0.5 mL
Vanilla	1/2 tsp.	2 mL
Hard margarine (or butter), melted	2 tbsp.	30 mL

Crêpes: Put all 9 ingredients into blender. Process until smooth. Add more orange juice, if necessary, to make thin batter. Chill for 1 hour. Heat small greased non-stick frying pan on medium until hot. Add about 2 tbsp. (30 mL) batter, quickly tilting pan to coat bottom. Cook for 30 seconds until edges start to brown and top loses its shine. Remove to waxed paper to cool. Repeat with remaining batter. Makes 20 crêpes.

Cottage Cheese Filling: Mash cottage cheese and egg yolk together until large curds are broken up.

Add next 5 ingredients. Mix well. Makes 2 1/2 cups (625 mL) filling. Spoon 1 1/2 tbsp. (25 mL) down center on unbrowned side of each crêpe. Fold 2 sides towards center, not overlapping. Roll from front to back to enclose filling. Arrange blintzes in single layer, seam side down, in greased shallow 9 x 13 inch (22 x 33 cm) baking dish.

Drizzle with margarine. Cover. Bake in 400°F (205°C) oven for 25 to 30 minutes until hot. Makes 20 blintzes.

1 blintz: 101 Calories; 4.2 g Total Fat; 114 mg Sodium; 7 g Protein; 9 g Carbohydrate; trace Dietary Fiber

Pictured on page 35.

Cheese And Honey

A soft whey cheese, such as Manouri or Manoypi, is often
served like this for breakfast in Greece. We tried it with readily available
low-fat quark cheese for a delicious and almost authentic alternative.
Also delicious paired with fresh berries or sliced fruit.

Liquid honey	1 – 2 tbsp.	15 – 30 mL
Low-fat quark cheese	1/3 cup	75 mL
Coarsely chopped walnuts (optional)	1 – 2 tsp.	5 – 10 mL

Drizzle honey over cheese in small dish. Stir gently just to marble honey through cheese. Sprinkle with walnuts. Serves 1.

1 serving: 146 Calories; 3.6 g Total Fat; 320 mg Sodium; 10 g Protein; 20 g Carbohydrate; 0 g Dietary Fiber

CINNAMON CHEESE AND HONEY: Omit walnuts. Add a sprinkle of ground cinnamon. Stir.

Welsh Rarebit

This toasted cheese makes an unusual and tasty appetizer or lunch dish.

Grated sharp Cheddar cheese (about 8 oz., 225 g)	2 cups	500 mL
All-purpose flour	1 tbsp.	15 mL
Beer	1/3 cup	75 mL
Dry mustard	1 1/2 tsp.	7 mL
Fresh bread slices, toasted	4	4

Toss cheese with flour in heavy medium saucepan. Add beer and mustard. Heat on very low, stirring often, until cheese is melted and smooth. (May be prepared to this point and reheated later.)

Place toasted bread slices on small greased baking sheet. Spoon cheese mixture over toast, completely covering surface. Broil 4 inches (10 cm) from heat until bubbly and lightly browned. Broiling for too long will make cheese tough. Makes 4 rarebits.

1 rarebit: 358 Calories; 21.2 g Total Fat; 583 mg Sodium; 19 g Protein; 22 g Carbohydrate; trace Dietary Fiber

Cheeseburger Pie

Lots of meat! Slight bite with nice oregano and basil flavor.

CRUST

All-purpose flour	1 1/2 cups	375 mL
Baking powder	2 tsp.	10 mL
Granulated sugar	1 tsp.	5 mL
Salt	1/2 tsp.	2 mL
Milk	1/2 cup	125 mL

FILLING

Lean ground beef	1 1/2 lbs.	680 g
Finely chopped onion	1/2 cup	125 mL
Grated medium Cheddar cheese (about 4 oz., 113 g)	1 cup	250 mL
Salsa	3/4 cup	175 mL
Dried whole oregano	1 tsp.	5 mL
Dried sweet basil	1/2 tsp.	2 mL
Salt	1 tsp.	5 mL
Pepper	1/4 tsp.	1 mL

TOPPING

Grated part-skim mozzarella cheese (about 4 oz., 113 g)	1 cup	250 mL

Crust: Combine flour, baking powder, sugar and salt in medium bowl. Add milk. Stir until soft dough forms. Turn out onto lightly floured surface. Knead 8 times. Roll out and press into greased 9 inch (22 cm) pie plate.

Filling: Scramble-fry ground beef and onion in frying pan until beef is no longer pink. Drain.

Add next 6 ingredients. Stir. Turn into crust.

Topping: Sprinkle mozzarella cheese over top. Bake in 350°F (175°C) oven for about 30 minutes until crust is golden. Cuts into 6 wedges.

1 wedge: 453 Calories; 20.3 g Total Fat; 1095 mg Sodium; 35 g Protein; 31 g Carbohydrate; 2 g Dietary Fiber

Cottage Roll

A nice sweet, soft loaf with a hint of orange.

FILLING

Boiling water	1/4 cup	60 mL
Instant rice	1/4 cup	60 mL
Dry curd cottage cheese	2 cups	500 mL
Granulated sugar	1 1/2 tbsp.	25 mL
Salt	1/2 tsp.	2 mL
Large egg	1	1
Freshly grated orange peel	1/2 – 1 tsp.	2 – 5 mL
Hard margarine (or butter)	1 1/2 tsp.	7 mL

DOUGH

All-purpose flour	1 3/4 cups	425 mL
Baking powder	2 tsp.	10 mL
Salt	1/4 tsp.	1 mL
Granulated sugar	1 tbsp.	15 mL
Spreadable cream cheese	3 tbsp.	50 mL
Cooking oil	2 tbsp.	30 mL
Milk	1/2 cup	125 mL

Filling: Stir water and rice together in small saucepan. Simmer, uncovered, for about 1 minute until tender. Cool.

Mix next 6 ingredients in medium bowl. Add rice. Stir.

Dough: Combine all 7 ingredients in medium bowl until dough pulls away from sides of bowl. Turn out onto lightly floured surface. Knead 6 times. Roll out to 11 x 14 inch (28 x 35 cm) rectangle. Spread filling in even layer to within 1/2 inch (12 mm) of edge. Roll up, jelly roll-style, from long side. Pinch seam and ends to seal. Place, seam side down, on greased baking sheet. Bake in 375°F (190°C) oven for 35 to 40 minutes until golden. Cut diagonally into eighteen 3/4 inch (2 cm) slices.

1 slice: 106 Calories; 3.3 g Total Fat; 161 mg Sodium; 5 g Protein; 14 g Carbohydrate; trace Dietary Fiber

Pictured on page 35.

SAVORY COTTAGE ROLL: Omit orange peel and 1 tsp. (5 mL) sugar from filling. Add 1/2 tsp. (2 mL) seasoned salt, 1/4 tsp. (1 mL) dill weed and 3 tbsp. (50 mL) spreadable garlic herb cream cheese.

Cheesy Rounds

Great to serve with Cauliflower Cheese Soup, page 142.

Grated medium Cheddar cheese (about 4 oz., 113 g)	1 cup	250 mL
Hard margarine (or butter), softened	1 tbsp.	15 mL
Dry mustard	1/4 tsp.	1 mL
Salt	1/8 tsp.	0.5 mL
Pepper, sprinkle		
English muffins, split (buttered, optional)	2	2
Tomato slices, 1/4 inch (6 mm) thick	4	4
Pepper, sprinkle		
Paprika, sprinkle		

Combine first 5 ingredients in small bowl.

Divide and spread cheese mixture on muffin halves. Top each with tomato slice. Sprinkle second amount of pepper and paprika over top. Arrange in single layer on ungreased baking sheet. Bake in 400°F (205°C) oven for 12 to 14 minutes until cheese is bubbly. Makes 4 rounds.

1 round: 240 Calories; 13.8 g Total Fat; 440 mg Sodium; 11 g Protein; 19 g Carbohydrate; 1 g Dietary Fiber

Scrambled Western

Loaded version of scrambled eggs. Lots of bacon and cheese flavor.

Bacon slices, cut into 3/4 inch (2 cm) pieces	10	10
Chopped onion	1/2 cup	125 mL
Chopped green pepper	1/2 cup	125 mL
Chopped green onion	2 tbsp.	30 mL
Chopped fresh parsley (or 1 1/2 tsp., 7 mL, flakes)	2 tbsp.	30 mL
Large eggs, fork-beaten	8	8

(continued on next page)

Grated medium Cheddar cheese (about 4 oz., 113 g)	1 cup	250 mL

Fry bacon in frying pan until almost crisp. Drain, leaving 1 tbsp. (15 mL) drippings in frying pan. Leave bacon in frying pan.

Add onion and green pepper. Sauté until onion is soft.

Add green onion and parsley. Sauté for 2 minutes.

Add eggs. Cook and stir until egg is cooked but still slightly soft.

Add cheese. Stir for about 1 minute until cheese is melted. Serves 4.

1 serving: 404 Calories; 31 g Total Fat; 565 mg Sodium; 25 g Protein; 5 g Carbohydrate; 1 g Dietary Fiber

Pictured on page 35.

Quesadillas

These kay-sah-DEE-yahs are quick and easy. They are so good you may want to make extra. Serve with salsa and sour cream.

Grated Monterey Jack cheese (about 3 oz., 85 g)	3/4 cup	175 mL
Flour tortillas (9 inch, 22 cm, size)	3	3
Finely chopped green onion	1 tbsp.	15 mL
Finely chopped celery	1 1/2 tbsp.	25 mL
Finely chopped red pepper	3 tbsp.	50 mL
Canned diced green chilies, finely chopped (optional)	1 tbsp.	15 mL
Hard margarine (or butter)	1 tbsp.	15 mL

Divide and sprinkle cheese over 1/2 of each tortilla to within about 1/2 inch (12 mm) of edge.

Divide and sprinkle next 4 ingredients over top.

Melt 1 tsp. (5 mL) margarine in frying pan on medium-high. Fold tortilla in half. Carefully transfer to frying pan. Brown 1 side. Carefully turn over. Brown other side. Repeat with remaining margarine and tortillas. Makes 3 quesadillas, each cutting into 4 wedges, for a total of 12 wedges. Serves 2.

1 serving: 430 Calories; 23.9 g Total Fat; 616 mg Sodium; 17 g Protein; 37 g Carbohydrate; 2 g Dietary Fiber

Quick Cheese Strata

Very cheesy. Very pretty. Very easy!

Bread slices, cut into 1/2 inch (12 mm) cubes	6	6
Grated medium Cheddar cheese (about 4 oz., 113 g)	1 cup	250 mL
Large eggs	3	3
Milk	1 1/4 cups	300 mL
Salt	1/2 tsp.	2 mL
Pepper	1/8 tsp.	0.5 mL

Put bread cubes into greased 1 1/2 quart (1.5 L) casserole. Sprinkle with cheese.

Beat eggs in medium bowl until frothy. Add milk, salt and pepper. Beat. Pour over cheese and bread cubes. Set casserole in larger baking pan with hot water coming up to 1 inch (2.5 cm) on sides. Bake, uncovered, in 325°F (160°C) oven for about 1 1/4 hours until set. Serves 4.

1 serving: 310 Calories; 15.9 g Total Fat; 771 mg Sodium; 18 g Protein; 23 g Carbohydrate; 1 g Dietary Fiber

Tex-Mex Strata

Delightful bean and corn combo. Serve with salsa.

Day-old bread slices, crusts removed	16	16
Can of kernel corn, drained	12 oz.	341 mL
Cans of diced green chilies (4 oz., 113 mL, each), with liquid	2	2
Can of black beans, drained and rinsed	14 oz.	398 mL
Grated Monterey Jack cheese (about 8 oz., 225 g)	2 cups	500 mL
Large eggs	6	6
Milk	3 cups	750 mL
Onion salt	1/2 tsp.	2 mL
Cayenne pepper	1/2 tsp.	2 mL
Salt	1/2 tsp.	2 mL
Pepper	1/8 tsp.	0.5 mL
Sliced ripe olives (optional), for garnish	2 tbsp.	30 mL
Medium tomato, diced, for garnish	1	1

(continued on next page)

Brunch

Fit 1/2 of bread slices into bottom of greased 9 × 13 inch (22 × 33 cm) pan. Layer with corn, chilies, beans and cheese. Fit remaining bread slices over top.

Beat eggs in medium bowl until frothy. Add next 5 ingredients. Beat on low until mixed. Carefully pour over bread slices. Cover. Chill for several hours or overnight. Bake in 350°F (175°C) oven for about 60 minutes until golden.

Sprinkle olives and tomato over top. Serves 8.

1 serving: 412 Calories; 16 g Total Fat; 1092 mg Sodium; 23 g Protein; 45 g Carbohydrate; 3 g Dietary Fiber

Pictured on page 35.

Cheese Sandwiches

Everyone who tries these interesting looking little wafer sandwiches will come back for more.

WAFERS

Grated sharp Cheddar cheese (about 4 oz., 113 g)	1 cup	250 mL
All-purpose flour	1 1/4 cups	300 mL
Cayenne pepper	1/8 tsp.	0.5 mL
Salt	1/8 tsp.	0.5 mL
Hard margarine (or butter)	1/4 cup	60 mL
Milk	3 tbsp.	50 mL

FILLING

Grated Swiss (or provolone) cheese (about 3 oz., 85 g)	1 cup	250 mL
Salad dressing (such as Miracle Whip)	1/4 cup	60 mL

Wafers: Measure first 4 ingredients into medium bowl. Cut in margarine until crumbly.

Drizzle milk over top. Stir with fork until ball forms. Roll into log 6 inches (15 cm) in length and about 1 1/2 inches (3.8 cm) in diameter. Chill. Cut into 1/4 inch (6 mm) thick slices. Arrange on ungreased baking sheets. Bake in 450°F (230°C) oven for 7 minutes until golden. Cool. Makes 24 wafers.

Filling: Mix Swiss cheese and salad dressing well in small bowl. Spread 1 1/2 tsp. (7 mL) on each of 12 wafers. Place remaining wafers on top. Heat in 450°F (230°C) oven for about 5 minutes until hot. Serve immediately. Makes 12 sandwiches.

1 sandwich: 190 Calories; 12.7 g Total Fat; 194 mg Sodium; 7 g Protein; 12 g Carbohydrate; trace Dietary Fiber

Stuffing Crust Quiche

So flavorful—mushrooms and cheese with a nip!

Finely chopped onion	3/4 cup	175 mL
Finely chopped celery	1/2 cup	125 mL
Hard margarine (or butter)	3 tbsp.	50 mL
Coarsely chopped fresh mushrooms	2 cups	500 mL
Hot water	1/3 cup	75 mL
Chicken bouillon powder	2 tsp.	10 mL
Parsley flakes	2 tsp.	10 mL
Dried sage, crushed	1/2 tsp.	2 mL
Pepper	1/8 tsp.	0.5 mL
Day-old whole wheat bread slices, torn into 1/2 inch (12 mm) pieces	3	3
Hard margarine (or butter)	1 tbsp.	15 mL
Cooked mixed vegetables (such as corn, peas, carrots, beans)	1 cup	250 mL
Grated Monterey Jack With Jalapeño cheese (about 6 oz., 170 g)	2 cups	500 mL
Large eggs	3	3
Creamed cottage cheese	1 cup	250 mL
Salt	1/2 tsp.	2 mL
Parsley flakes	1/2 tsp.	2 mL
Paprika	1/2 tsp.	2 mL
Cayenne pepper	1/4 tsp.	1 mL

Sauté onion and celery in first amount of margarine in frying pan until onion is soft. Add mushrooms. Sauté until liquid from mushrooms has evaporated and onion is soft. Remove from heat.

Add hot water, bouillon powder, first amount of parsley flakes, sage and pepper. Stir well. Add bread. Toss until bread is evenly moistened.

Grease 10 inch (25 cm) glass pie plate with second amount of margarine. Press bread mixture into bottom and up sides of pie plate.

Scatter vegetables and Monterey Jack cheese over bread mixture.

(continued on next page)

Put remaining 6 ingredients into food processor or blender. Process until puréed. Pour over cheese. Bake, uncovered, on center rack in 325°F (160°C) oven for about 50 minutes until knife inserted in center comes out mostly clean. Let stand for 10 minutes before cutting. Cuts into 8 wedges.

1 wedge: 275 Calories; 18.7 g Total Fat; 748 mg Sodium; 16 g Protein; 12 g Carbohydrate; 2 g Dietary Fiber

Pictured on page 36.

Mushroom Quiche

*Whether in a pie shell or mini-tart shells, mushrooms
and onion are always a welcome flavor combo.*

Grated Swiss cheese (about 4 oz., 113 g)	1 cup	250 mL
Grated medium Cheddar cheese (about 2 oz., 57 g)	1/2 cup	125 mL
Can of mushroom stems and pieces, drained	10 oz.	284 mL
All-purpose flour	1/4 cup	60 mL
Salt	1/2 tsp.	2 mL
Pepper	1/4 tsp.	1 mL
Unbaked 9 inch (22 cm) pie shell	1	1
Large eggs	4	4
Green onions, finely chopped (about 1/4 cup, 60 mL)	2	2
Half-and-half cream (or homogenized milk)	1 cup	250 mL
Worcestershire sauce	1 tsp.	5 mL
Cayenne pepper	1/8 tsp.	0.5 mL

Toss first 6 ingredients together in medium bowl. Scatter evenly over bottom of pie shell.

Beat eggs until frothy. Add green onion, cream, Worcestershire sauce and cayenne pepper. Stir. Pour over cheese mixture. Bake in 350°F (175°C) oven for about 55 minutes until set and golden. Let stand for 10 minutes before cutting. Cuts into 6 wedges.

1 wedge: 347 Calories; 23.2 g Total Fat; 615 mg Sodium; 15 g Protein; 19 g Carbohydrate; 1 g Dietary Fiber

Variation: Omit pie shell. Use sixteen 3 inch (7.5 cm) frozen tart shells, thawed. Spoon 1 1/2 tbsp. (25 mL) filling into each shell.

Pictured on page 36.

Brunch

Blue Onion Pie

Use your favorite blue cheese in this rich brunch or luncheon pie.

Large eggs, fork-beaten until frothy	3	3
Ricotta cheese	1 cup	250 mL
Homogenized milk	3/4 cup	175 mL
Sliced green onion	1/2 cup	125 mL
Chopped fresh parsley (or 1 1/2 tsp., 7 mL, flakes)	2 tbsp.	30 mL
Salt	1/2 tsp.	2 mL
Freshly ground pepper, sprinkle		
Unbaked 9 inch (22 cm) pie shell	1	1
Blue cheese (such as Stilton, Roquefort, Gorgonzola or Danish Blue), broken up	4 oz.	113 g

Combine first 7 ingredients in medium bowl. Pour into pie shell.

Sprinkle blue cheese evenly over egg mixture. Bake on bottom rack in 350°F (175°C) oven for about 50 minutes until golden. Let stand for 10 minutes before cutting. Cuts into 8 wedges.

1 wedge: 233 Calories; 16.2 g Total Fat; 512 mg Sodium; 11 g Protein; 11 g Carbohydrate; trace Dietary Fiber

Pictured on page 36.

Burger Quiche

Tasty, economical and simple to prepare. This will soon become a family favorite.

Lean ground beef	1 lb.	454 g
Finely chopped onion	1/4 cup	60 mL
Light mayonnaise	1/2 cup	125 mL
Milk	1/2 cup	125 mL
All-purpose flour	1 tbsp.	15 mL
Large eggs	3	3
Parsley flakes	1/2 tsp.	2 mL
Grated medium Cheddar cheese (about 4 oz., 113 g)	1 cup	250 mL
Grated part-skim mozzarella cheese (about 2 oz., 57 g)	1/2 cup	125 mL
Unbaked 9 inch (22 cm) pie shell	1	1

(continued on next page)

Grated Parmesan cheese	3 tbsp.	50 mL

Scramble-fry ground beef and onion in frying pan until beef is no longer pink and onion is soft. Remove from heat. Drain well.

Gradually stir mayonnaise and milk into flour in small bowl until smooth. Add eggs and parsley flakes. Mix well. Add to beef mixture. Stir.

Scatter Cheddar and mozzarella cheeses evenly over bottom of pie shell. Pour beef mixture over cheeses.

Sprinkle Parmesan cheese over top. Bake in 350°F (175°C) oven for 35 to 40 minutes until set. Let stand for 10 minutes before cutting. Cuts into 6 wedges.

1 wedge: 462 Calories; 31.7 g Total Fat; 587 mg Sodium; 27 g Protein; 16 g Carbohydrate; trace Dietary Fiber

Pictured on front cover.

Chicken Quiche

Soft, creamy and rich. Muenster cheese comes through nicely.

Chopped cooked chicken	1 cup	250 mL
Unbaked 9 inch (22 cm) pie shell	1	1
Grated Muenster (or Havarti) cheese (about 4 oz., 113 g)	1 cup	250 mL
Large eggs, fork-beaten	3	3
Can of condensed cream of chicken soup	10 oz.	284 mL
Onion powder	1/4 tsp.	1 mL
Chopped fresh chives (or 1 1/2 tsp., 7 mL, dried)	2 tbsp.	30 mL
Parsley flakes	1 tsp.	5 mL
Dill weed	1/2 tsp.	2 mL
Milk	3/4 cup	175 mL
Pepper	1/8 tsp.	0.5 mL

Scatter chicken over bottom of pie shell. Sprinkle cheese over top.

Stir remaining 8 ingredients together in medium bowl until well mixed. Pour over cheese. Bake in 350°F (175°C) oven for about 55 minutes until knife inserted near center comes out clean. Let stand for 10 minutes before cutting. Cuts into 6 wedges.

1 wedge: 310 Calories; 18.4 g Total Fat; 729 mg Sodium; 19 g Protein; 17 g Carbohydrate; trace Dietary Fiber

Pictured on page 36.

Coffee Cheesecake

A slightly lower-in-fat cheesecake. Wonderful coffee flavor with chocolate crumb crust.

CRUST

Hard margarine (or butter)	6 tbsp.	100 mL
Graham cracker crumbs	1 cup	250 mL
Cocoa, sifted if lumpy	1/4 cup	60 mL
Instant coffee granules, crushed to fine powder	1/2 tsp.	2 mL
Granulated sugar	1/4 cup	60 mL

FILLING

Block of non-fat cream cheese, softened	8 oz.	250 g
Block of light cream cheese, softened	8 oz.	250 g
Instant coffee granules, crushed to fine powder	1 1/2 tsp.	7 mL
Granulated sugar	2/3 cup	150 mL
Large eggs	2	2
Light sour cream	1/3 cup	75 mL
Chopped pecans (or walnuts), optional	1/3 cup	75 mL

TOPPING

Boiling water	1 tbsp.	15 mL
Instant coffee granules	1 1/2 tsp.	7 mL
Light sour cream	1/2 cup	125 mL
Brown sugar, packed	2 tsp.	10 mL
Whipped cream, for garnish	1 cup	250 mL
Chocolate-covered coffee beans, for garnish	8	8

Crust: Melt margarine in medium saucepan. Stir in graham crumbs, cocoa, instant coffee powder and granulated sugar until well mixed. Press into ungreased 8 inch (20 cm) springform pan. Set aside.

Filling: Beat both cream cheeses, instant coffee powder and granulated sugar together in large bowl until smooth. Beat in eggs, 1 at a time, on low until just mixed.

Add sour cream and pecans. Stir. Pour over crust. Bake in 350°F (175°C) oven for about 55 minutes until set. Remove to wire rack.

(continued on next page)

Desserts

Topping: Stir boiling water into instant coffee powder in small bowl. Add sour cream and brown sugar. Stir. Spread over cheesecake. Bake for 10 minutes. Run knife around side to allow cheesecake to settle evenly. Cool. Remove side of pan. Chill for several hours or overnight.

Garnish with whipped cream and coffee beans. Cuts into 8 wedges.

1 wedge: 370 Calories; 19.4 g Total Fat; 415 mg Sodium; 9 g Protein; 43 g Carbohydrate; 1 g Dietary Fiber

Pictured on page 53 and on back cover.

Chocolate Cheesecake

So good when served with dabs of whipped cream and chocolate cutouts.
Always better on the second day.

CHOCOLATE WAFER CRUST

Hard margarine (or butter)	1/3 cup	75 mL
Chocolate wafer crumbs	1 1/2 cups	375 mL
Granulated sugar	2 tbsp.	30 mL

FILLING

Blocks of light cream cheese, softened (8 oz., 250 g, each)	3	3
Granulated sugar	3/4 cup	175 mL
Cocoa, sifted if lumpy	1/2 cup	125 mL
Light sour cream	1/2 cup	125 mL
Large eggs	3	3
Vanilla	1 1/2 tsp.	7 mL

Chocolate Wafer Crust: Melt margarine in medium saucepan. Stir in wafer crumbs and sugar until well mixed. Press into bottom and halfway up sides of ungreased 10 inch (25 cm) springform pan. Bake in 350°F (175°C) oven for 10 minutes.

Filling: Beat cream cheese, sugar and cocoa together in large bowl until smooth.

Add sour cream. Beat until well mixed. Beat in eggs, 1 at a time, on low until just mixed. Add vanilla. Mix. Pour into and spread evenly in crust. Bake in 350°F (175°C) oven for 50 to 55 minutes until outside is set and center is slightly jiggly. Remove to wire rack. Run knife around side to allow cheesecake to settle evenly. Cool at room temperature. Chill. Remove side of pan. Cuts into 12 wedges.

1 wedge: 350 Calories; 22.1 g Total Fat; 605 mg Sodium; 9 g Protein; 31 g Carbohydrate; 1 g Dietary Fiber

Pictured on page 53 and on back cover.

Cottage Cheesecake

Very soft and sweet rum-flavored cheesecake.

CRUST

Hard margarine (or butter)	1/4 cup	60 mL
Graham cracker crumbs	1 1/4 cups	300 mL
Brown sugar, packed	1/4 cup	60 mL

FILLING

Large eggs	3	3
Creamed cottage cheese, smoothed in blender (or sieved)	3 cups	750 mL
Brown sugar, packed	1 cup	250 mL
All-purpose flour	2 tbsp.	30 mL
Salt	1/2 tsp.	2 mL
Vanilla	1 tsp.	5 mL
Rum flavoring	1/2 tsp.	2 mL

Crust: Melt margarine in medium saucepan. Stir in graham crumbs and brown sugar until well mixed. Reserve 1/2 cup (125 mL). Press remaining crumb mixture into ungreased 9 x 9 inch (22 x 22 cm) pan. Bake in 350°F (175°C) oven for 10 minutes.

Filling: Beat eggs in medium bowl until frothy. Add remaining 6 ingredients. Beat until smooth. Pour evenly over crust. Sprinkle reserved crumb mixture over top. Bake for about 40 minutes until set. Cuts into 12 pieces.

1 piece: 248 Calories; 8.8 g Total Fat; 452 mg Sodium; 9 g Protein; 33 g Carbohydrate; trace Dietary Fiber

Pictured on page 53.

1. Chocolate Cheesecake, page 51
2. Lemon Cheesecake, page 55
3. Coffee Cheesecake, page 50
4. Blueberry Cheesecake, page 57
5. Cottage Cheesecake, above

Props Courtesy Of: Linens 'N Things
Sears Canada Inc.
Stokes

Lemon Cheesecake

This easy cake-mix cheesecake actually tastes like a lighter textured cheesecake. Serve plain or with a dab of your favorite pie filling.

Yellow cake mix (2 layer size)	1	1
Cooking oil	1/4 cup	60 mL
Large egg	1	1
Blocks of cream cheese (8 oz., 250 g, each), softened	2	2
Can of sweetened condensed milk	11 oz.	300 mL
Large eggs	3	3
Lemon juice	1/4 cup	60 mL
Grated lemon peel	2 tsp.	10 mL
Vanilla	1 tsp.	5 mL

Reserve 1/2 cup (125 mL) cake mix. Mix remaining cake mix, cooking oil and first egg in large bowl. Press into bottom and halfway up sides of greased 9 × 13 inch (22 × 33 cm) pan.

Beat cream cheese and condensed milk together in medium bowl until smooth.

Beat in remaining eggs, 1 at a time. Add reserved cake mix, lemon juice, lemon peel and vanilla. Beat to mix. Pour into crust. Bake in 300°F (150°C) oven for about 50 minutes until wooden pick inserted in center comes out clean. Cool. Chill. Cuts into 16 pieces.

1 piece: 381 Calories; 21.7 g Total Fat; 354 mg Sodium; 7 g Protein; 40 g Carbohydrate; trace Dietary Fiber

Pictured on page 53 and on back cover.

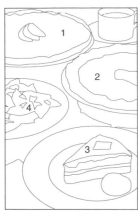

1. Blue Cheese Pear Pizza, page 58
2. Cheddar Pastry Apple Pie, page 56
3. Mascarpone Mocha Dessert, page 66
4. Viennese Pastries, page 69

Props Courtesy Of: The Bay

Cheddar Pastry Apple Pie

Cheddar and apple are always a great combination. Makes a very large pie.

CHEDDAR PASTRY

All-purpose flour	1 1/2 cups	375 mL
Whole wheat flour	3/4 cup	175 mL
Salt	3/4 tsp.	4 mL
Cold lard (or shortening)	3/4 cup	175 mL
Grated sharp Cheddar cheese (about 5 oz., 140 g)	1 1/4 cups	300 mL
Large egg	1	1
White vinegar	2 tsp.	10 mL
Cold water	3 – 4 tbsp.	50 – 60 mL

FILLING

Granulated sugar	1 cup	250 mL
All-purpose flour	1/4 cup	60 mL
Ground cinnamon (optional)	1/4 – 1/2 tsp.	1 – 2 mL
Tart medium cooking apples (such as Granny Smith), peeled, cored and cut into 1/4 inch (6 mm) slices (about 8 cups, 2 L)	7	7
Grated sharp Cheddar cheese (about 4 oz., 113 g)	1 cup	250 mL

Cheddar Pastry: Combine both flours and salt in large bowl. Cut in lard and cheese until mixture is crumbly.

Fork-beat egg and vinegar together in small dish. Pour over flour mixture. Stir gently with fork. Gradually add cold water, 1 tbsp. (15 mL) at a time, while tossing and stirring with fork until flour is moistened and dough clings together. Form 2 balls, 1 slightly larger than the other. Flatten slightly into discs. Wrap in plastic wrap. Chill for 1 hour. Turn larger disc out onto lightly floured surface. Roll out to circle, about 1/8 inch (3 mm) thick and 12 inches (30 cm) in diameter. Handling dough carefully to prevent tearing, transfer to 10 inch (25 cm) pie plate, leaving edges overhanging.

Filling: Combine sugar, flour and cinnamon in large bowl. Add apples. Toss to coat well. Turn into pie shell.

(continued on next page)

Scatter cheese evenly over top. Dampen edge of pie shell with water. Roll out remaining disc to 11 inch (28 cm) circle. Fit over bottom crust. Press edge together all around. Trim edges, leaving 1/2 inch (12 mm) overhang. Turn or roll edges under. Crimp to seal. Cut slits in top or cut apple shape out of center of top crust. Use scraps to make leaf. Place on crust near cutout. Bake on bottom rack in 375°F (190°C) oven for about 1 hour until apples are tender. Cover with foil if crust gets too dark too quickly. Cuts into 10 pieces.

1 piece: 514 Calories; 26.4 g Total Fat; 352 mg Sodium; 11 g Protein; 60 g Carbohydrate; 4 g Dietary Fiber

Pictured on page 54.

Blueberry Cheesecake

No baking required for this yummy treat. Garnish with whipped cream.

GRAHAM CRUST

Hard margarine (or butter)	1/3 cup	75 mL
Graham cracker crumbs	1 1/2 cups	375 mL
Brown sugar, packed	1/4 cup	60 mL

FILLING

Envelope of dessert topping (not prepared)	1	1
Milk	1/2 cup	125 mL
Block of cream cheese	8 oz.	250 g
Icing (confectioner's) sugar	1 cup	250 mL
Almond flavoring	1 tsp.	5 mL
Can of blueberry pie filling	19 oz.	540 mL

Graham Crust: Melt margarine in medium saucepan. Stir in graham crumbs and brown sugar until well mixed. Press firmly into ungreased 9 x 9 inch (22 x 22 cm) pan.

Filling: Combine dessert topping and milk in small bowl. Beat on low until just moistened. Beat on high until stiff peaks form.

Using same beaters, beat cream cheese, icing sugar and almond flavoring together in medium bowl until smooth and light. Fold in dessert topping mixture. Spread evenly over crust. Chill for at least 3 hours or overnight.

Stir pie filling. Spoon dabs over individual servings. Cuts into 12 pieces.

1 piece: 308 Calories; 15.4 g Total Fat; 207 mg Sodium; 3 g Protein; 41 g Carbohydrate; 1 g Dietary Fiber

Pictured on page 53 and on back cover.

Blue Cheese Pear Pizza

An elegant, not-too-sweet dessert with a pleasant mild blue cheese taste.
The pears are enhanced by the mild tang of the cheese.

Dry boxed pastry mix for 2 crust pie	1	1
Crumbled blue cheese (such as Stilton or Gorgonzola), about 3 oz. (85 g)	2/3 cup	150 mL
Cold water	4 - 5 tbsp.	60 - 75 mL
Firm ripe pears, peeled, cored and sliced into 1/4 inch (6 mm) wedges	6	6
Block of cream cheese, softened	4 oz.	125 g
Large egg	1	1
Granulated sugar	1/2 cup	125 mL
All-purpose flour	1 tbsp.	15 mL
Vanilla	1 tsp.	5 mL

Combine pastry mix and cheese in medium bowl. Gradually add water, 1 tbsp. (15 mL) at a time, until dough forms a ball. Reserve 1/4 of dough. Press remaining dough in ungreased 12 inch (30 cm) pizza pan, forming small rim around edge.

Arrange pears over crust in spiral pattern starting at center.

Beat remaining 5 ingredients in medium bowl until smooth. Spoon over pears. Carefully spread evenly. Roll out reserved dough. Make cutouts as desired. Arrange over cream cheese mixture. Bake on bottom rack in 375°F (190°C) oven for about 35 minutes until golden and set. Cuts into 10 wedges.

1 wedge: 286 Calories; 15.9 g Total Fat; 342 mg Sodium; 5 g Protein; 32 g Carbohydrate; 2 g Dietary Fiber

Pictured on page 54.

Paré Pointer
If a frog's car breaks down, he just gets it toad away.

Desserts

Cream Cheese Cookies

Crispy on the outside and soft on the inside.

Block of cream cheese, softened	8 oz.	250 g
Hard margarine (or butter), softened	1/4 cup	60 mL
Vanilla	1/2 tsp.	2 mL
Yellow (or white) cake mix (2 layer size)	1	1
Chopped walnuts	1/2 cup	125 mL

Beat cream cheese, margarine and vanilla together in medium bowl until smooth.

Gradually add cake mix, in 3 additions, mixing well after each addition.

Add walnuts. Mix. Drop by level teaspoonfuls onto greased cookie sheet. Bake in 350°F (175°C) oven for 18 minutes. Makes about 4 dozen cookies.

1 cookie: 86 Calories; 5 g Total Fat; 104 mg Sodium; 1 g Protein; 9 g Carbohydrate; trace Dietary Fiber

Cheese Cookies

Pale yellow, crispy and very buttery. Great served with tea or fresh fruit.

Hard margarine (or butter), softened	1 cup	250 mL
Granulated sugar	1/2 cup	125 mL
Large egg	1	1
Grated sharp Cheddar cheese (6 oz., 170 g)	1 1/2 cups	375 mL
All-purpose flour	2 cups	500 mL
Baking powder	1 tsp.	5 mL
Salt	1/4 tsp.	1 mL

Cream margarine, sugar and egg in large bowl.

Add cheese. Beat well.

Add flour, baking powder and salt. Mix. Shape into 1 inch (2.5 cm) balls. Arrange about 1 inch (2.5 cm) apart on ungreased cookie sheet. Press with floured fork. Bake in 350°F (175°C) oven for 20 minutes. Makes about 4 dozen cookies.

1 cookie: 78 Calories; 5.2 g Total Fat; 88 mg Sodium; 2 g Protein; 6 g Carbohydrate; trace Dietary Fiber

Chocolate Cream Cheese Cake

Not a cheesecake but cheesy nonetheless. Creamy, chocolaty icing.

Hard margarine (or butter), softened	1/2 cup	125 mL
Block of cream cheese, softened	4 oz.	125 g
Icing (confectioner's) sugar	3 cups	750 mL
Milk	3 tbsp.	50 mL
Unsweetened chocolate baking squares (1 oz., 28 g, each), melted	4	4
Vanilla	1/2 tsp.	2 mL
Large eggs	3	3
All-purpose flour	2 1/4 cups	550 mL
Baking powder	1 tsp.	5 mL
Baking soda	1 tsp.	5 mL
Salt	1 tsp.	5 mL
Milk	1 cup	250 mL

CHOCO CHEESE ICING

Block of cream cheese, softened	4 oz.	125 g
Hard margarine (or butter), softened	1/4 cup	60 mL
Unsweetened chocolate baking squares (1 oz., 28 g, each), melted	2	2
Icing (confectioner's) sugar	2 1/2 cups	625 mL
Water	3 tbsp.	50 mL
Vanilla	1/2 tsp.	2 mL

Combine first 7 ingredients in large bowl. Beat until smooth and fluffy.

Mix flour, baking powder, baking soda and salt in small bowl.

Add flour mixture to cream cheese mixture in 3 additions, alternating with milk in 2 additions, beginning and ending with flour mixture. Turn into 2 greased 9 inch (22 cm) round pans. Bake in 350°F (175°C) oven for about 30 minutes until wooden pick inserted in center comes out clean. Let stand in pan for 15 minutes before turning out onto wire racks to cool.

Choco Cheese Icing: Beat all 6 ingredients together in medium bowl until smooth. Add more water or icing sugar as needed to make proper spreading consistency. Smooth between cake layers. Ice top and sides. Cuts into 16 wedges.

1 wedge: 451 Calories; 21.7 g Total Fat; 428 mg Sodium; 6 g Protein; 62 g Carbohydrate; 2 g Dietary Fiber

Cherry Pound Cake

Because of the firm texture of a pound cake, you have more slices to serve.
Moist and flavorful.

Block of cream cheese, softened	8 oz.	250 g
Granulated sugar	1/3 cup	75 mL
Cooking oil	1/2 cup	125 mL
Large eggs	3	3
White cake mix (2 layer size)	1	1
Jar of maraschino cherries, well drained and syrup reserved	9 oz.	250 mL
CHERRY GLAZE		
Icing (confectioner's) sugar, approximately	1 cup	250 mL
Maraschino cherry syrup	1 tbsp.	15 mL
Lemon juice, approximately	1 tbsp.	15 mL

Beat cream cheese, granulated sugar and cooking oil together in medium bowl until smooth. Beat in eggs, 1 at a time.

Add cake mix. Beat on low until just moistened.

Stir in cherries. Turn into greased 12 cup (3 L) bundt pan. Bake in 350°F (175°C) oven for about 55 minutes until wooden pick inserted in center comes out clean. Let stand for 20 minutes. Remove to wire rack to cool.

Cherry Glaze: Mix icing sugar, cherry syrup and lemon juice in small bowl, adding more icing sugar or lemon juice until barely pourable consistency. Drizzle over cooled cake. Cuts into 20 pieces.

1 piece: 261 Calories; 13.7 g Total Fat; 221 mg Sodium; 3 g Protein; 32 g Carbohydrate; trace Dietary Fiber

BLUEBERRY POUND CAKE: Omit cherries. Add 1 cup (250 mL) fresh (or frozen, thawed) blueberries.

 Freeze cheese in no more than 1 lb. (454 g) pieces. Larger pieces take a long time to freeze, which increases their tendency to be very crumbly when thawed.

Cream Cheese Icing

Smooth, creamy and everybody's favorite. Spreads well.

Block of cream cheese, softened	8 oz.	250 g
Hard margarine (or butter), softened	1/4 cup	60 mL
Icing (confectioner's) sugar	4 cups	1 L
Vanilla	1 1/2 tsp.	7 mL

Beat all 4 ingredients together well in medium bowl, adding more icing sugar as needed to make proper spreading consistency, until smooth and light. Makes 2 3/4 cups (675 mL).

1 tbsp. (15 mL): 72 Calories; 3 g Total Fat; 29 mg Sodium; trace Protein; 11 g Carbohydrate; 0 g Dietary Fiber

CHOCOLATE CHEESE ICING: Beat in 1/2 cup (125 mL) cocoa. Makes about 3 cups (750 mL).

Lemon Cheese Icing

A pale yellow, thick and creamy icing. Silky smooth.
Makes enough to ice and fill a double layer cake.

Block of cream cheese, softened	8 oz.	250 g
Icing (confectioner's) sugar	1 cup	250 mL
Instant lemon pudding powder (4 serving size)	1	1
Milk	1 cup	250 mL
Lemon juice	1 tsp.	5 mL
Frozen whipped topping, thawed	2 cups	500 mL

Beat cream cheese and icing sugar together in medium bowl until smooth.

Add pudding powder, milk and lemon juice. Beat on low for about 2 minutes until smooth.

Fold in whipped topping. Makes about 4 cups (1 L).

1 tbsp. (15 mL): 36 Calories; 2 g Total Fat; 36 mg Sodium; trace Protein; 4 g Carbohydrate; 0 g Dietary Fiber

Choco Cream Cheese Icing

A light chocolate color—looks good on a dark chocolate cake.
Creamy smooth. Makes enough to ice a double layer cake.
Use with Cream Cheese Brownies, page 64.

Block of cream cheese, softened	8 oz.	250 g
Semisweet chocolate chips, melted	1/2 cup	125 mL
Milk	2 tbsp.	30 mL
Vanilla	1 tsp.	5 mL
Icing (confectioner's) sugar	4 cups	1 L

Beat cream cheese, chocolate, milk and vanilla together well in medium bowl. Add icing sugar, 1 cup (250 mL) at a time, beating well after each addition, adding more milk or icing sugar as needed to make proper spreading consistency. Makes about 3 cups (750 mL).

1 tbsp. (15 mL): 66 Calories; 2.3 g Total Fat; 15 mg Sodium; trace Protein; 11 g Carbohydrate; trace Dietary Fiber

Cream Cheese Fudge

Mild chocolate flavor, creamy and sweet. Softer than traditional fudge.

Block of cream cheese, softened	8 oz.	250 g
Icing (confectioner's) sugar	4 cups	1 L
Semisweet chocolate chips, melted	2/3 cup	150 mL
Chopped walnuts	1 1/2 cups	375 mL

Beat cream cheese and icing sugar together in medium bowl until smooth.

Stir in chocolate and walnuts. Spread in foil-lined 8 × 8 inch (20 × 20 cm) pan. Chill. Cuts into 64 squares.

1 square: 72 Calories; 3.7 g Total Fat; 12 mg Sodium; 1 g Protein; 10 g Carbohydrate; trace Dietary Fiber

Cream Cheese Brownies

Chocolate and cream cheese—great combo!

Block of non-fat cream cheese	8 oz.	250 g
Large egg	1	1
Granulated sugar	1/3 cup	75 mL
All-purpose flour	2 tbsp.	30 mL
Vanilla	1/2 tsp.	2 mL
Semisweet chocolate chips, melted	2/3 cup	150 mL
Hard margarine (or butter)	1/2 cup	125 mL
Cocoa, sifted if lumpy	1/4 cup	60 mL
Large eggs	2	2
Granulated sugar	3/4 cup	175 mL
All-purpose flour	3/4 cup	175 mL
Vanilla	1 tsp.	5 mL
Salt	1/8 tsp.	0.5 mL
Chopped walnuts	1/2 cup	125 mL

Choco Cream Cheese Icing, page 63
(1/2 recipe)

Beat cream cheese, first egg, first amounts of sugar, flour and vanilla together in small bowl until smooth. Fold in chocolate.

Combine margarine and cocoa in small saucepan. Heat and stir until smooth. Cool.

Beat remaining 2 eggs in medium bowl until frothy. Add second amounts of sugar, flour, vanilla and salt. Beat.

Add walnuts and cocoa mixture. Stir. Spread about 2/3 of cocoa mixture into greased 9 × 9 inch (22 × 22 cm) pan. Spoon dabs of cream cheese mixture here and there over cocoa mixture. Spread as best you can with tip of knife. Drop about 1/2 tsp.(2 mL) dabs of remaining cocoa mixture in rows on cream cheese mixture. When baked and iced, this will look fine. Bake in 350°F (175°C) oven for 30 to 35 minutes until wooden pick inserted in center comes out moist but clean. Cool.

Spread icing over top. Cuts into 36 squares.

1 square: 157 Calories; 8.2 g Total Fat; 105 mg Sodium; 3 g Protein; 20 g Carbohydrate; 1 g Dietary Fiber

Lazy Blintz

Sweet crunchy crust and subtle lemon flavor with a wonderful creamy texture.
Serve with a fruit topping.

FILLING

Ricotta cheese	4 cups	1 L
Block of cream cheese, softened	8 oz.	250 g
Large eggs	2	2
Granulated sugar	1/3 cup	75 mL
Lemon juice	1/4 cup	60 mL
Salt	1/8 tsp.	0.5 mL

CRUST

Hard margarine (or butter), softened	1 cup	250 mL
Granulated sugar	1/2 cup	125 mL
Large eggs	2	2
Milk	1/4 cup	60 mL
Vanilla	1 tsp.	5 mL
All-purpose flour	1 cup	250 mL
Baking powder	1 tbsp.	15 mL
Salt	1/8 tsp.	0.5 mL

Filling: Beat all 6 ingredients together in large bowl until smooth.

Crust: Beat all 8 ingredients in medium bowl until well mixed. Spread 1/2 in greased 9 x 13 inch (22 x 33 cm) pan. Add filling. Drop dabs of remaining crust batter here and there over filling to cover as best you can. Crust will smooth out as it bakes. Bake in 325°F (160°C) oven for 50 to 55 minutes until golden and sides start to pull away from sides of pan. Cuts into 15 pieces.

1 piece: 395 Calories; 29.2 g Total Fat; 393 mg Sodium; 12 g Protein; 22 g Carbohydrate; trace Dietary Fiber

Paré Pointer

Your vacation doesn't have to be long for you to come back short.

Mascarpone Mocha Dessert

Buttery-rich Mascarpone cheese is what makes tiramisu desserts so delicious.

Cocoa	2 tsp.	10 mL
Cold prepared triple strength coffee (or espresso)	1/3 cup	75 mL
Hazelnut-flavored liqueur (such as Frangelico) or other nut, coffee or chocolate-flavored liqueur (see Note)	1/3 cup	75 mL
Thick chocolate chip cookies, 2 1/2 inches (6.4 cm) in diameter	22	22
FILLING		
Egg yolks (large)	2	2
Granulated sugar	2 tbsp.	30 mL
Milk	1/4 cup	60 mL
Vanilla	1/2 tsp.	2 mL
Egg whites (large), room temperature	2	2
Granulated sugar	2 tbsp.	30 mL
Mascarpone cheese	8 oz.	225 g
Whipping cream	1 cup	250 mL
Envelope of unflavored gelatin (1/4 oz., 7 g)	1/2	1/2
Water	2 tbsp.	30 mL
Hot water	2 tbsp.	30 mL
Cocoa	2 tsp.	10 mL

Spray 8 inch (20 cm) springform pan with cooking spray. Sift cocoa onto sides and bottom.

Combine coffee and liqueur in small bowl. Divide evenly between two small bowls. Quickly dip 1/2 of cookies into 1/2 of coffee mixture. Arrange in single layer in pan.

Filling: Beat egg yolks and first amount of sugar in small heatproof bowl until very thick and light.

Beat in milk and vanilla. Place bowl over simmering water in small saucepan. Heat and stir until mixture is thickened and coats back of spoon. Cover with plastic wrap directly on surface to prevent skin from forming. Cool to room temperature.

(continued on next page)

Beat egg whites in medium bowl with clean beaters until frothy. Gradually beat in second amount of sugar until stiff and glossy.

Mash cheese with fork in large bowl. Fold egg white mixture into cheese.

Put egg yolk mixture into medium bowl. Add whipping cream. Beat until very soft peak stage.

Sprinkle gelatin over water in separate small bowl. Let stand for 1 minute. Stir. Add hot water. Stir until dissolved. Fold whipped cream and gelatin mixtures into cheese mixture. Layer 1/2 of filling over cookies.

Sift 1/2 of cocoa over filling. Quickly dip remaining cookies into remaining coffee mixture. Arrange in single layer over filling. Cover with remaining filling. Dust with remaining cocoa. Chill, uncovered, for several hours or overnight. Serves 8 to 10.

1 serving: 431 Calories; 26.9 g Total Fat; 214 mg Sodium; 13 g Protein; 31 g Carbohydrate; 1 g Dietary Fiber

Pictured on page 54.

Note: For an alcohol-free dessert, omit liqueur. Use same amount of milk.

Cheese Squares

Very nice subtle vanilla flavor. Simple yet good.

VANILLA WAFER CRUST

Hard margarine (or butter)	2/3 cup	150 mL
Vanilla wafer crumbs	2 1/2 cups	625 mL
Brown sugar, packed	1/4 cup	60 mL

FILLING

Blocks of cream cheese (8 oz., 250 g, each), softened	2	2
Large eggs	2	2
Granulated sugar	2/3 cup	150 mL
Lemon juice	3 tbsp.	50 mL
Vanilla	1 tsp.	5 mL

Vanilla Wafer Crust: Melt margarine in medium saucepan. Stir in wafer crumbs and brown sugar until well mixed. Reserve 1/4 cup (60 mL). Press remaining crumbs into ungreased 9 x 13 inch (22 x 33 cm) pan. Bake in 350°F (175°C) oven for 10 to 15 minutes until golden. Cool.

Filling: Beat all 5 ingredients in small bowl until smooth. Spread over crust. Sprinkle reserved crumbs over top. Bake for about 25 minutes until set. Cool. Cuts into 24 pieces.

1 piece: 199 Calories; 14.4 g Total Fat; 158 mg Sodium; 3 g Protein; 16 g Carbohydrate; trace Dietary Fiber

Sweet Dessert Kugel

Traditionally served on the Jewish Sabbath, this baked noodle pudding with dried fruit is the sweet version. Comfort food at its best.

Medium egg noodles	2 1/2 cups	625 mL
Boiling water	6 cups	1.5 L
Salt	1 1/2 tsp.	7 mL
Spreadable cream cheese	1/4 cup	60 mL
Creamed cottage cheese	1/2 cup	125 mL
Granulated sugar	1/4 cup	60 mL
Salt	1/4 tsp.	1 mL
Hard margarine (or butter), melted	2 tbsp.	30 mL
Large eggs	3	3
Milk	1/2 cup	125 mL
Vanilla yogurt	1 cup	250 mL
Mixed dried fruit (such as apricots, blueberries, cherries, cranberries, peaches, raisins), chopped	1/2 cup	125 mL
Grated Colby (or mild Cheddar) cheese (about 4 oz., 113 g)	1 cup	250 mL
Shortbread cookies, processed into crumbs	1/3 cup	75 mL

Cook noodles in boiling water and first amount of salt in large uncovered saucepan for 7 to 9 minutes, stirring occasionally, until tender but firm. Drain. Rinse well with cold water. Drain well. Turn into greased 1 1/2 quart (1.5 L) casserole.

Put cream cheese, cottage cheese, sugar, second amount of salt and margarine into blender or food processor. Process until fine texture and almost smooth.

Add eggs, 1 at a time, processing briefly after each addition. Pour over noodles.

Add milk and yogurt. Stir until well combined.

Add dried fruit and Colby cheese. Stir until well mixed.

Sprinkle cookie crumbs over top. Bake, uncovered, in 350°F (175°C) oven for 1 hour until outside is set and center is slightly jiggly. Serves 6 to 8.

1 serving: 435 Calories; 21.3 g Total Fat; 484 mg Sodium; 17 g Protein; 45 g Carbohydrate; 1 g Dietary Fiber

Viennese Pastries

So pretty on a plate with other dainties. The rich, puffy pastry can also be used to make Curried Mushroom And Feta Tarts, page 13.

CREAM CHEESE PASTRY

All-purpose flour	2 cups	500 mL
Block of cream cheese, chilled	8 oz.	250 g
Butter (not margarine), chilled	1 cup	250 mL
Thick jam (your choice)	1/2–2/3 cup	125–150 mL
Milk	1 tbsp.	15 mL
Egg white (large), fork-beaten	1	1
Coarse sugar (or finely crushed hazelnuts or other crushed nuts)	1 tbsp.	15 mL

Cream Cheese Pastry: Blend flour, cream cheese and butter with pastry cutter in large bowl until mixture can be formed into a ball. Cover with plastic wrap. Chill for at least 2 hours. Divide dough into 2 equal portions. Roll out, 1 portion at a time, to 1/8 inch (3 mm) thickness on lightly floured surface. To keep pastry tender, avoid adding too much flour when rolling out. Cut into 3 inch (7.5 cm) squares.

Place 1/2 to 3/4 tsp. (2 to 4 mL) jam in center of each square. Make 1 inch (2.5 cm) diagonal cut in each corner (see Figure 1, below). Dampen alternating corners with milk. Bring dampened corners to center in pinwheel design (see Figure 2, below). Press lightly together to seal.

Lightly brush pastry with egg white. Sprinkle with coarse sugar. Arrange in single layer 2 inches (5 cm) apart on greased baking sheet. Bake on bottom rack in 375°F (190°C) oven for 12 to 15 minutes until golden. Makes 36 pastries.

1 pastry: 112 Calories; 7.9 g Total Fat; 79 mg Sodium; 1 g Protein; 9 g Carbohydrate; trace Dietary Fiber

Pictured on page 54.

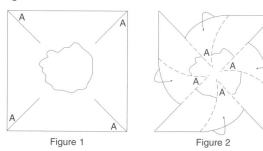

Figure 1   Figure 2

Caramelized Pears And Cheese

The flavor of the sweet pears mellows the sharp Stilton cheese.
If Stilton cheese is not your thing, any strong cheese, such as Gorgonzola,
sharp Cheddar, Parmesan or Romano, will work well.

Lemon juice	2 tbsp.	30 mL
Water	1/4 cup	60 mL
Firm ripe pears, peeled, halved and cored	4	4
Butter (not margarine)	2 tbsp.	30 mL
Granulated sugar	2 tbsp.	30 mL
Grated (or crumbled) Stilton cheese	1 - 2 tbsp.	15 - 30 mL

Combine lemon juice and water in small bowl.

Cut pears crosswise into about 1/2 inch (12 mm) thick slices. Add to lemon juice mixture. Stir to coat completely.

Melt butter in large frying pan. Drain pears. Add to frying pan. Sprinkle with sugar. Stir gently. Cook on medium for about 9 minutes, stirring occasionally, until sugar caramelizes on both sides and pears are tender. Divide among individual dessert plates. Drizzle with pan liquid.

Divide and sprinkle cheese over hot pears. Serve immediately. Serves 4.

1 serving: 130 Calories; 6.5 g Total Fat; 93 mg Sodium; 1 g Protein; 19 g Carbohydrate;
3 g Dietary Fiber

1. Pepper And Mushroom Pizza, page 88
2. Rotini Rosé, page 79
3. Bruschetta Melt, page 80

Cheesed-Off Apples

Cheddar crumb topping over tender, sweet apples.

Medium cooking apples (such as McIntosh), peeled, cored and sliced (about 6 1/2 cups, 1.6 L)	7	7
Granulated sugar	3/4 cup	175 mL
Lemon juice	1 tbsp.	15 mL
TOPPING		
All-purpose flour	1 cup	250 mL
Granulated sugar	1/3 cup	75 mL
Salt	1/4 tsp.	1 mL
Hard margarine (or butter), softened	6 tbsp.	100 mL
Grated sharp Cheddar cheese (about 4 oz., 113 g)	1 cup	250 mL

Put apples into ungreased 3 quart (3 L) casserole. Sprinkle sugar over top. Drizzle with lemon juice.

Topping: Combine flour, sugar and salt in medium bowl. Cut in margarine until crumbly.

Add cheese. Stir. Scatter over apples. Gently press down. Bake in 350°F (175°C) oven for about 60 minutes until apples are tender. Serves 6.

1 serving: 478 Calories; 18.8 g Total Fat; 359 mg Sodium; 8 g Protein; 73 g Carbohydrate; 3 g Dietary Fiber

1. Light Tiramisu, page 74
2. Caramel Cheesecake, page 76
3. Light Lemon Cheesecake, page 75

Props Courtesy Of: Linens 'N Things
The Bay

Light Tiramisu

Nice touch of cheese, chocolate and coffee. Creamy and sweet.

Cold water	2 tbsp.	30 mL
Hazelnut-flavored liqueur (such as Frangelico)	1/3 cup	75 mL
Envelope of unflavored gelatin	1/4 oz.	7 g
Low-fat ricotta cheese	1 cup	250 mL
Quark (or ricotta) cheese	1 cup	250 mL
Block of light cream cheese, softened, cut up	8 oz.	250 g
Vanilla	1 tsp.	5 mL
Egg whites (large), room temperature	3	3
Brown sugar, packed	1/2 cup	125 mL
Instant coffee granules (or espresso instant coffee granules)	1 1/2 tsp.	7 mL
Boiling water	1/3 cup	75 mL
Giant ladyfingers (or 15 regular-size ladyfingers)	10	10

Cocoa, for garnish

Combine cold water and liqueur in small saucepan. Sprinkle gelatin over top. Let stand for 1 minute. Heat and stir on low until gelatin is dissolved. Remove from heat. Cool to warm room temperature, but do not allow to set.

Put ricotta cheese and gelatin mixture into blender. Process until smooth. Add quark cheese, cream cheese and vanilla. Process until smooth.

Beat egg whites in large bowl until frothy. Slowly add brown sugar, 1 tbsp. (15 mL) at a time, until sugar is dissolved and stiff peaks form. Fold cheese mixture into egg white mixture until well mixed and no white streaks remain.

Dissolve instant coffee granules in boiling water in small cup. Cool.

Arrange 1/2 of ladyfingers in single layer in bottom of 8 cup (2 L) glass bowl. Drizzle with 1/2 of coffee. Cover with 1/2 of cheese mixture. Repeat with remaining ladyfingers, coffee and cheese mixture.

Sift cocoa over top. Chill for at least 1 1/2 hours. Serves 6.

1 serving: 441 Calories; 15.9 g Total Fat; 583 mg Sodium; 19 g Protein; 47 g Carbohydrate; 0 g Dietary Fiber

Pictured on page 72.

Light Lemon Cheesecake

For lemon lovers who want a few less calories in their dessert.

CRUST

Hard margarine (or butter)	3 tbsp.	50 mL
Vanilla wafer crumbs	1 1/2 cups	375 mL
Lemon juice	1 tbsp.	15 mL
Lemon zest	1 tsp.	5 mL

FILLING

Boiling water	2 cups	500 mL
Packages of lemon-flavored gelatin (jelly powder), 3 oz. (85 g) each	2	2
Cold water	1 cup	250 mL
Block of non-fat cream cheese	8 oz.	250 g
Light sour cream	1 cup	250 mL
Granulated sugar	1/3 cup	75 mL
Lemon zest	2 tsp.	10 mL
Lemon juice	1 tbsp.	15 mL
Vanilla	1 tsp.	5 mL

Crust: Melt margarine in medium saucepan. Stir in wafer crumbs, lemon juice and lemon zest until well mixed. Reserve 2 tbsp. (30 mL) crumbs. Press remaining crumbs into ungreased 9 inch (22 cm) springform pan.

Filling: Stir boiling water and gelatin in medium bowl until dissolved. Add cold water. Chill, stirring and scraping down sides often, until thick and syrupy.

Beat remaining 6 ingredients together in separate medium bowl until smooth. Stir into gelatin mixture. Pour over crust. Sprinkle with reserved crumbs. Chill. Cuts into 12 wedges.

1 wedge: 188 Calories; 6 g Total Fat; 112 mg Sodium; 4 g Protein; 31 g Carbohydrate; trace Dietary Fiber

Pictured on page 72.

 Low-fat cheese does not melt as quickly as cheese with a higher fat content. To reduce fat and calories you may want to use less cheese in a recipe rather than use low-fat cheese. The taste will be about the same but the texture will be superior.

Caramel Cheesecake

An awesome dessert that will fill any craving you might have.

CRUST

Hard margarine (or butter)	3 tbsp.	50 mL
Graham cracker crumbs	1 cup	250 mL
Brown sugar, packed	1 tbsp.	15 mL
Milk	1 1/2 tbsp.	25 mL

FILLING

Blocks of non-fat cream cheese (8 oz., 250 g, each)	2	2
Low-fat ricotta cheese	1 cup	250 mL
Brown sugar, packed	3/4 cup	175 mL
All-purpose flour	3 tbsp.	50 mL
Large eggs	2	2
Vanilla	1 tsp.	5 mL

TOPPING

Non-fat sour cream	1 cup	250 mL
Brown sugar, packed	3/4 cup	175 mL
Vanilla	1/2 tsp.	2 mL
All-purpose flour	2 tbsp.	30 mL

Crust: Melt margarine in medium saucepan. Stir in graham crumbs, brown sugar and milk until well mixed. Press into bottom of 8 inch (20 cm) springform pan. Bake in 350°F (175°C) oven for 10 minutes. Cool.

Filling: Beat first 4 ingredients together in medium bowl until smooth.

Beat in eggs, 1 at a time, until just blended. Add vanilla. Mix. Pour over crust. Spread evenly. Bake for about 50 minutes until set.

Topping: Beat all 4 ingredients together in small bowl. Spread over filling. Bake for 10 minutes. Cool. Chill for several hours or overnight. Cuts into 12 pieces.

1 piece: 346 Calories; 14.3 g Total Fat; 421 mg Sodium; 8 g Protein; 45 g Carbohydrate; trace Dietary Fiber

Pictured on page 72.

Cheesy Squares

Graham cracker crust with a light lemon filling.

BOTTOM LAYER

Hard margarine (or butter)	6 tbsp.	100 mL
Graham cracker crumbs	1 1/2 cups	375 mL
Brown sugar, packed	2 tbsp.	30 mL

TOP LAYER

Envelope of unflavored gelatin	1/4 oz.	7 g
Water	1/4 cup	60 mL
Blocks of light cream cheese, softened	8 oz.	250 g
Freshly squeezed lemon juice (about 2 small)	5 tbsp.	75 mL
Can of sweetened condensed milk	11 oz.	300 mL
Frozen whipped topping, thawed	2 cups	500 mL

Bottom Layer: Melt margarine in medium saucepan. Add graham crumbs and brown sugar. Stir until well mixed. Reserve 1/3 cup (75 mL) crumb mixture. Press remaining crumb mixture into ungreased 9 × 13 inch (22 × 33 cm) baking pan. Bake in 350°F (175°C) oven for 10 minutes. Cool.

Top Layer: Sprinkle gelatin over water in small saucepan. Let stand for 1 minute. Heat and stir on low until gelatin is dissolved. Cool to warm room temperature, but do not allow to set.

Beat cream cheese, lemon juice and condensed milk together in large bowl until smooth. Add gelatin. Beat well.

Fold in whipped topping. Pour over crust. Sprinkle reserved crumb mixture over top. Chill until firm. Cuts into 15 pieces.

1 piece: 231 Calories; 12.9 g Total Fat; 270 mg Sodium; 5 g Protein; 25 g Carbohydrate; trace Dietary Fiber

Paré Pointer

He wanted the man's daughter's hand in marriage,
but her father said he had to take all of her or nothing.

Easy Cheesy Noodles

Using a process creamy cheese makes this dish very rich tasting.
It will remind you of lasagne.

Broad egg noodles	8 oz.	225 g
Boiling water	10 cups	2.5 L
Salt	2 tsp.	10 mL
Lean ground beef	1 lb.	454 g
Chopped onion	1/2 cup	125 mL
Garlic clove, minced (or 1/4 tsp., 1 mL, powder)	1	1
Jar of spaghetti sauce (your choice)	24 oz.	680 mL
Pasteurized cheese loaf, cubed (such as Velveeta)	9 oz.	250 g
Grated mozzarella cheese (about 6 oz., 170 g)	1 1/2 cups	375 mL

Cook noodles in boiling water and salt in large uncovered saucepan for 5 to 7 minutes until tender but firm. Drain. Rinse. Place in ungreased 2 quart (2 L) casserole.

Scramble-fry ground beef, onion and garlic in frying pan until beef is no longer pink and onion is soft. Drain.

Add spaghetti sauce and pasteurized cheese. Stir until cheese is melted. Pour over noodles.

Sprinkle with mozzarella cheese. Bake, uncovered, in 350°F (175°C) oven for about 30 minutes until hot and cheese is golden. Serves 6.

1 serving: 639 Calories; 33.5 g Total Fat; 1349 mg Sodium; 36 g Protein; 48 g Carbohydrate; 3 g Dietary Fiber

 To use frozen cheese, thaw slowly in the refrigerator, preferably for twenty-four hours or longer.

Rotini Rosé

A thick cheesy mushroom sauce coats tender rotini pasta.
Slightly lower in fat but not in taste.

Rotini pasta (about 10 oz., 285 g)	4 cups	1 L
Boiling water	12 cups	3 L
Salt	1 tbsp.	15 mL
Garlic clove, minced (or 1/4 tsp., 1 mL, powder)	1	1
Sliced fresh mushrooms	1 cup	250 mL
Hard margarine (or butter)	1 tbsp.	15 mL
Green onions, chopped	2	2
Can of tomato sauce	7 1/2 oz.	213 mL
Dried sweet basil	1/2 tsp.	2 mL
Dried whole oregano	1/2 tsp.	2 mL
Salt, sprinkle		
Freshly ground pepper, sprinkle		
Frozen egg product, thawed (or 4 large eggs)	8 oz.	227 mL
Skim evaporated milk	1 cup	250 mL
Grated light sharp Cheddar cheese (about 6 oz., 170 g)	1 1/2 cups	375 mL
Grated light Parmesan cheese	1/4 cup	60 mL

Cook pasta in boiling water and salt in large uncovered pot or Dutch oven for about 12 minutes until tender but firm. Drain. Rinse well with cold water. Drain well. Return to pot.

Sauté garlic and mushrooms in margarine in large frying pan for about 3 minutes until liquid from mushrooms has evaporated.

Add green onion. Stir. Cook for about 2 minutes until mushrooms are golden.

Add next 5 ingredients. Cook, uncovered, on medium-low for 5 minutes. Add to pasta. Stir.

Combine egg product and evaporated milk in small bowl. Stir into pasta mixture.

Add both cheeses. Stir. Heat on medium until sauce thickens and pasta is coated. Serve immediately. Makes 6 1/4 cups (1.5 L).

1 cup (250 mL): 356 Calories; 9.5 g Total Fat; 609 mg Sodium; 23 g Protein; 44 g Carbohydrate; 2 g Dietary Fiber

Pictured on page 71.

Bruschetta Melt

You can have the cheese—without the guilt! Add a slice of fat-reduced deli-style chicken or pastrami on top of tomato mixture for even more of a treat.

Fat-free Italian salad dressing	2 tbsp.	30 mL
Non-fat mayonnaise (not salad dressing)	1 tbsp.	15 mL
Garlic clove, minced (or 1/4 tsp., 1 mL, powder)	1	1
Chopped fresh sweet basil (or 3/4 tsp., 4 mL, dried)	1 tbsp.	15 mL
Salt	1/8 tsp.	0.5 mL
Freshly ground pepper, sprinkle		
Large roma (plum) tomato, seeded and diced (about 2/3 cup, 150 mL)	1	1
Grated part-skim mozzarella cheese (about 2 oz., 57 g)	1/2 cup	125 mL
Grated light Parmesan cheese	1 tbsp.	15 mL
Sourdough bread slices, 1/2 inch (12 mm) thick	4	4
Olive (or cooking) oil	1 tbsp.	15 mL

Combine first 9 ingredients in small bowl. Makes 1 cup (250 mL) tomato mixture.

Lightly brush 1 side of bread slices with 1/2 of olive oil. Divide tomato mixture on oiled side of 2 bread slices. Cover with remaining 2 bread slices, oiled side down. Press down slightly. Brush remaining olive oil on outside of bread slices. Grill in large non-stick frying pan on medium for about 3 minutes per side until bread is toasted and cheese is melted. Makes 2 sandwiches.

1 sandwich: 364 Calories; 14.6 g Total Fat; 1010 mg Sodium; 16 g Protein; 43 g Carbohydrate; 3 g Dietary Fiber

Pictured on page 71.

 For easier shredding or grating of soft cheese, first place in the freezer for 15 to 20 minutes until very firm.

Greek Cheese Pastries

Delicate, buttery pastry encloses a cheese and tomato filling.
These freeze very well before or after baking.

CHEESE FILLING

Garlic herb cream cheese, softened	4 oz.	125 g
Goat's milk feta cheese, crumbled (about 1 1/4 cups, 300 mL)	8 oz.	225 g
Finely grated Greek Myzithra cheese (about 4 oz., 113 g)	1 cup	250 mL
Large eggs, fork-beaten	2	2
Chopped ripe olives (optional)	3 tbsp.	50 mL
Chopped fresh parsley (or 1 tsp., 5 mL, flakes)	1 1/2 tbsp.	25 mL
Chopped fresh oregano leaves (or 1/4 tsp., 1 mL, dried)	1 tsp.	5 mL
Chopped sun-dried dry-pack tomatoes (about 1 oz., 28 g), softened in boiling water for 10 minutes before chopping	1/3 cup	75 mL
Hard margarine (or butter), melted	3 tbsp.	50 mL
Olive (or cooking) oil	3 tbsp.	50 mL
Frozen phyllo pastry sheets, thawed according to package directions	12	12

Cheese Filling: Mash cream cheese in medium bowl until smooth. Add next 6 ingredients. Stir.

Add tomato to cheese mixture. Stir. Makes 2 1/3 cups (575 mL) filling.

Combine margarine and olive oil in small dish. Lay 1 phyllo sheet vertically on work surface. Cover remaining phyllo sheets with damp tea towel to prevent drying out. Brush phyllo sheet lightly with margarine mixture. Fold sheet lengthwise into thirds. Place 3 tbsp. (50 mL) filling in center at 1 end. Fold 1 corner diagonally towards straight edge to form triangle. Continue folding back and forth in same fashion, enclosing filling. Arrange, smooth side up, on ungreased baking sheet. Repeat with remaining phyllo sheets and filling. Bake in 375°F (190°C) oven for about 15 minutes until golden and flaky. Makes 12 cheese pastries.

1 cheese pastry: 245 Calories; 18.2 g Total Fat; 541 mg Sodium; 8 g Protein; 13 g Carbohydrate; 0 g Dietary Fiber

Pictured on page 89.

Variation: To bake from frozen state, bake in 375°F (190°C) oven for 20 to 25 minutes until golden and flaky.

Spinach And Cheese Croquettes

A crisp crust surrounds a creamy surprise.

Green onions, sliced	2	2
Frozen chopped spinach, thawed and squeezed dry	10 oz.	300 g
Hard margarine (or butter)	1/3 cup	75 mL
All-purpose flour	7/8 cup	200 mL
Salt	1 1/2 tsp.	7 mL
Dried marjoram	1/2 tsp.	2 mL
Dried crushed chilies	1/2 tsp.	2 mL
Pepper, sprinkle		
Milk	2 1/2 cups	625 mL
Fine dry bread crumbs	2 1/2 cups	625 mL
Large eggs	3	3
Milk	1/3 cup	75 mL
Sticks of sharp Cheddar (or Monterey Jack, Gouda, Edam or Swiss) cheese, 1/2 × 3 inch (1.2 × 7.5 cm) size, chilled	16	16

Cooking oil, for deep-frying

Sauté green onion and spinach in margarine for 3 minutes until liquid from spinach has evaporated.

Combine flour, salt, marjoram, chilies and pepper in large saucepan. Slowly stir in first amount of milk until smooth. Heat and stir on medium until boiling and very thick. Add spinach mixture. Stir. Pour into ungreased 9 × 13 inch (22 × 33 cm) pan. Cover with plastic wrap directly on surface to prevent skin forming. Chill for several hours or overnight. Turn out onto work surface. Remove plastic wrap or foil. Cut into 16 equal portions.

Place bread crumbs in shallow dish or pie plate.

Fork-beat eggs and second amount of milk together in shallow medium bowl. Carefully lift up 1 spinach mixture portion with spatula. Drop into bread crumbs.

Press 1 cheese stick into uncoated side of spinach mixture. Wrap spinach mixture around cheese stick to make cylindrical shape. Roll in bread crumbs to coat completely. Dip into egg mixture. Roll in bread crumbs again to coat completely. Repeat with remaining spinach mixture, bread crumbs and egg mixture. Chill, uncovered, on waxed paper-lined baking sheet for 1 to 2 hours.

(continued on next page)

Lunch

Deep-fry in hot (375°F, 190°C) cooking oil for 3 to 4 minutes, turning gently once or twice, until golden. Remove with slotted spoon to paper towels to drain. Makes 16 croquettes.

1 croquette: 239 Calories; 13 g Total Fat; 544 mg Sodium; 9 g Protein; 21 g Carbohydrate; 1 g Dietary Fiber

Pictured on page 89.

APPETIZER CROQUETTES: Cut cheese sticks in half lengthwise. Divide spinach mixture into 32 equal portions. Wrap spinach mixture around cheese sticks, either into cylindrical shape or into balls. Makes 32 appetizer croquettes.

Count Cristo Sandwich

Turkey and Gruyère cheese enclosed in French toast. Delicious!

Dijon mustard and mayonnaise sandwich spread (see Note)	4 tsp.	20 mL
White bread slices	2	2
Gruyère cheese slices	2	2
Shaved roast turkey slices	2	2
Freshly ground pepper, sprinkle		
Large egg	1	1
Milk	1 tbsp.	15 mL
Cooking oil	1 tsp.	5 mL
Hard margarine (or butter)	1 tsp.	5 mL

Spread sandwich spread on 1 side of each bread slice. Layer 1 cheese slice, turkey slice and remaining cheese slice on sandwich-spread side of 1 bread slice. Sprinkle pepper over top. Cover with remaining bread slice, sandwich-spread side down.

Fork-beat egg and milk together in small shallow dish, large enough to hold sandwich, until frothy. Dip sandwich into egg mixture. Turn over to coat completely.

Heat cooking oil and margarine in non-stick frying pan until bubbly. Place sandwich in frying pan. Cook on medium-low for about 5 minutes per side until browned. Makes 1 sandwich.

1 sandwich: 554 Calories; 33.8 g Total Fat; 715 mg Sodium; 34 g Protein; 27 g Carbohydrate; 1 g Dietary Fiber

Note: Combine 1 tsp. (5 mL) Dijon mustard and 1 tbsp. (15 mL) mayonnaise in small dish to substitute for commercial sandwich spread.

The Ultimate Grilled Cheese Sandwiches

Some exceptional variations of an old standby.
Of course, serving with ketchup is always optional!

BLONDE BOMBSHELL

Thinly sliced Asiago cheese	1 oz.	28 g
Bacon slices, cooked crisp and crumbled	2	2
Thinly sliced sharp Cheddar cheese	1 oz.	28 g
Caraway bread slices	2	2
Hard margarine (or butter), softened	1 tbsp.	15 mL

1 sandwich: 539 Calories; 35.6 g Total Fat; 1043 mg Sodium; 22 g Protein; 32 g Carbohydrate; 4 g Dietary Fiber

UKRAINIAN SNACK

Thinly sliced sharp Cheddar cheese	1 oz.	28 g
Garlic dill pickle, thinly sliced and blotted dry	1	1
Thinly sliced garlic ham sausage (such as kielbasa)	1 1/4 oz.	35 g
Thinly sliced sharp Cheddar cheese	1 oz.	28 g
Whole wheat bread slices	2	2
Hard margarine (or butter), softened	1 tbsp.	15 mL

1 sandwich: 545 Calories; 36.7 g Total Fat; 1948 mg Sodium; 26 g Protein; 31 g Carbohydrate; 5 g Dietary Fiber

TANGY TOMATO

Thinly sliced extra sharp Cheddar cheese	1 1/2 oz.	42 g
Medium roma (plum) tomato, sliced	1	1
Thinly sliced extra sharp Cheddar cheese	1 1/2 oz.	42 g
Sourdough bread slices	2	2
Hard margarine (or butter), softened	1 tbsp.	15 mL

1 sandwich: 603 Calories; 37.3 g Total Fat; 1008 mg Sodium; 25 g Protein; 43 g Carbohydrate; 3 g Dietary Fiber

(continued on next page)

BIG MAMA

Process cheese slice	1	1
Ketchup	2 tsp.	10 mL
Bacon slices, cooked crisp and crumbled	2	2
Process cheese slice	1	1
White bread slices	2	2
Hard margarine (or butter), softened	1 tbsp.	15 mL

1 sandwich: 478 Calories; 32.8 g Total Fat; 1328 mg Sodium; 18 g Protein; 28 g Carbohydrate; 1 g Dietary Fiber

AA TRIPLE DECKER

Grated light sharp Cheddar cheese (about 1 1/3 oz., 37 g)	1/3 cup	75 mL
Thin rye bread slice	1	1
Grated part-skim mozzarella cheese (about 1 1/3 oz., 37 g)	1/3 cup	75 mL
Thin rye bread slices	2	2
Hard margarine (or butter), softened	1 tbsp.	15 mL

1 sandwich: 460 Calories; 22.5 g Total Fat; 1089 mg Sodium; 27 g Protein; 37 g Carbohydrate; 4 g Dietary Fiber

SAMSOE AND BLACK FOREST HAM

Prepared mustard	1/2 tsp.	2 mL
Thinly sliced Samsoe cheese	1 1/2 oz.	42 g
Shaved Black Forest ham	3/4 oz.	21 g
Thinly sliced Samsoe cheese	1 1/2 oz.	42 g
Prepared mustard (optional)	1/2 tsp.	2 mL
Light rye bread slices	2	2
Hard margarine (or butter), softened	1 tbsp.	15 mL

1 sandwich: 547 Calories; 37 g Total Fat; 1027 mg Sodium; 29 g Protein; 24 g Carbohydrate; 3 g Dietary Fiber

(continued on next page)

SIESTA WAKE-UP CALL

Thinly sliced sharp Cheddar cheese	1 oz.	28 g
Pickled hot pepper rings, drained	4 - 6	4 - 6
Thinly sliced sharp Cheddar cheese	1 oz.	28 g
Whole wheat bread slices	2	2
Hard margarine (or butter), softened	1 tbsp.	15 mL

1 sandwich: 472 Calories; 32.6 g Total Fat; 946 mg Sodium; 20 g Protein; 28 g Carbohydrate; 4 g Dietary Fiber

SMOKY CHEESE AND HAM

Thinly sliced smoked Gouda cheese	1 1/2 oz.	42 g
Thinly sliced ham	3/4 oz.	21 g
Thinly sliced smoked Gouda cheese	1 1/2 oz.	42 g
Sourdough bread slices	2	2
Hard margarine (or butter), softened	1 tbsp.	15 mL

1 sandwich: 577 Calories; 34.3 g Total Fat; 1447 mg Sodium; 28 g Protein; 38 g Carbohydrate; 2 g Dietary Fiber

FOR MUSHROOM LOVERS

Thinly sliced Swiss cheese	1 oz.	28 g
Sautéed sliced mushrooms (see Note)	1/2 cup	125 mL
Thinly sliced Swiss cheese	1 oz.	28 g
Brown bread slices	2	2
Hard margarine (or butter), softened	1 tbsp.	15 mL

1 sandwich: 480 Calories; 31.4 g Total Fat; 604 mg Sodium; 22 g Protein; 30 g Carbohydrate; 4 g Dietary Fiber

Note: Sauté sliced mushrooms in 1/2 tsp. (2 mL) margarine in frying pan until golden and liquid from mushrooms has evaporated.

METHOD FOR ALL SANDWICHES: Layer or spread ingredients, in order given, on 1 bread slice. Cover with remaining bread slice.

Spread 1/2 of margarine on top bread slice. Place, buttered side down, in frying pan. Spread remaining margarine on top bread slice. Cook for 2 minutes per side on medium-high until golden and cheese is melted. Makes 1 sandwich.

Paré Pointer

If you see one thousand rabbits walking backwards, you are looking at a receding hare line.

Lunch

Cheesy Dill Pizza

A real medley of cheese and vegetables.

Biscuit mix	2 cups	500 mL
All-purpose flour	3 tbsp.	50 mL
Granulated sugar	1 tsp.	5 mL
Dill weed	1 1/2 tsp.	7 mL
Onion powder	1/2 tsp.	2 mL
Parsley flakes	1/2 tsp.	2 mL
Salt	1/4 tsp.	1 mL
Large egg	1	1
Creamed cottage cheese	2/3 cup	150 mL
Cooking oil	2 tbsp.	30 mL
TOPPING		
Grated carrot	1/2 cup	125 mL
Chopped celery	1/4 cup	60 mL
Chopped onion	1/4 cup	60 mL
Grated potato	1/2 cup	125 mL
Chopped fresh mushrooms	1/2 cup	125 mL
Dill weed	1/2 tsp.	2 mL
Salt	1/4 tsp.	1 mL
Pepper	1/16 tsp.	0.5 mL
Cooking oil	1 1/2 tsp.	7 mL
Water	2 tbsp.	30 mL
Dry curd cottage cheese	1/2 cup	125 mL
Grated sharp Cheddar cheese (about 4 oz., 113 g)	1 cup	250 mL

Measure first 7 ingredients into large bowl. Stir. Make a well in center.

Put egg, creamed cottage cheese and cooking oil into blender. Process until smooth. Pour into well. Stir until dough forms soft ball. Turn out onto lightly floured surface. Knead 8 times. Roll out and press in greased 12 inch (30 cm) pizza pan, forming rim around edge.

Topping: Combine first 10 ingredients in large frying pan. Heat until simmering. Cover. Steam for about 5 minutes until water has evaporated. Remove from heat.

Stir in dry curd cottage cheese. Makes 1 1/4 cups (300 mL) topping. Spread over crust.

Sprinkle with Cheddar cheese. Bake on bottom rack in 425°F (220°C) oven for about 20 minutes until cheese is melted and crust is golden. Cuts into 8 wedges.

1 wedge: 306 Calories; 15.6 g Total Fat; 833 mg Sodium; 12 g Protein; 29 g Carbohydrate; 1 g Dietary Fiber

Pepper And Mushroom Pizza

Good spicy flavor. No need to precook ingredients.

Can of pizza sauce	7 1/2 oz.	213 mL
Unbaked pizza crust (12 inch, 30 cm, size)	1	1
Finely sliced pepperoni (2 inch, 5 cm, diameter)	1 cup	250 mL
Sliced fresh mushrooms	1 cup	250 mL
Medium green pepper, sliced into strips	1	1
Grated part-skim mozzarella cheese (about 6 oz., 170 g)	1 1/2 cups	375 mL

Spread pizza sauce on crust. Layer pepperoni over sauce. Sprinkle mushrooms, green pepper and cheese over pepperoni. Bake on bottom rack in 425°F (220°C) oven for about 15 minutes until cheese is melted and crust is golden. Cuts into 8 wedges.

1 wedge: 317 Calories; 12.7 g Total Fat; 808 mg Sodium; 15 g Protein; 37 g Carbohydrate; 4 g Dietary Fiber

Pictured on page 71.

1. Greek Cheese Pastries, page 81
2. Spinach And Cheese Croquettes, page 82
3. Festive Chicken Sandwiches, page 91

Props Courtesy Of: Dansk Gifts

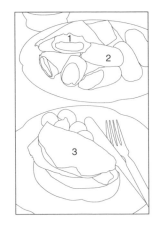

Festive Chicken Sandwiches

Delicately seasoned chicken topped with ham and cheese in buns.

All-purpose flour	1/3 cup	75 mL
Salt	1/2 tsp.	2 mL
Pepper	1/8 tsp.	0.5 mL
Paprika	1/4 tsp.	1 mL
Boneless, skinless chicken breast halves (about 1 lb., 454 g), pounded thin and cut in half	4	4
Cooking oil	2 tbsp.	30 mL
Deli ham slices, cut to almost fit chicken	5	5
Mozzarella cheese slices, cut to fit chicken	5	5
French bread slices (or 4 hamburger buns)	8	8

Combine flour, salt, pepper and paprika in shallow bowl or on waxed paper. Press chicken into flour mixture to coat completely.

Brown chicken on both sides in cooking oil in frying pan. Arrange in single layer on greased baking sheet.

Cover chicken with ham slices. Top each with 1 cheese slice. Bake in 350°F (175°C) oven for about 8 minutes until hot and cheese has melted.

Place 1 chicken portion on bread slice. Repeat with remaining chicken and bread slices. Serves 8.

1 serving: 393 Calories; 15.8 g Total Fat; 1308 mg Sodium; 34 g Protein; 27 g Carbohydrate; trace Dietary Fiber

Pictured on page 89.

1. Zucchini Cheese Pull-Aparts, page 27
2. Shelf Pasta, page 109
3. Three-Cheese Manicotti, page 118
4. Vermicelli Plate With Myzithra, page 119

Props Courtesy Of: Anchor Hocking Canada
Cherison Enterprises Inc.

Chili Pie

Chili and hot peppers add a nice bite to this dish.

Lean ground beef	1 1/2 lbs.	680 g
Medium onion, chopped	1	1
Can of condensed tomato soup	10 oz.	284 mL
Can of kernel corn, drained	12 oz.	341 mL
Can of diced tomatoes, with juice	14 oz.	398 mL
Chili powder	1 tbsp.	15 mL
Salt	1 tsp.	5 mL
Pepper	1/4 tsp.	1 mL
Can of sliced ripe olives, drained	4 1/2 oz.	125 mL
Grated longhorn (or Monterey Jack) cheese (about 4 oz., 113 g)	1 cup	250 mL
All-purpose flour	1 cup	250 mL
Baking powder	1 tsp.	5 mL
Salt	1/2 tsp.	2 mL
Grated sharp Cheddar cheese	1/2 cup	125 mL
Milk	3/4 cup	175 mL
Cooking oil	2 tbsp.	30 mL
Large egg	1	1
Finely chopped hot chili peppers (or 1/4 tsp., 1 mL, cayenne pepper)	1 tsp.	5 mL
Chili powder	1/2 tsp.	2 mL
Grated Monterey Jack cheese	1/2 cup	125 mL
Grated longhorn (or Monterey Jack) cheese	1/2 cup	125 mL

Scramble-fry ground beef and onion in large saucepan until beef is no longer pink. Drain.

Add next 7 ingredients. Stir. Turn into ungreased 3 quart (3 L) casserole.

Sprinkle first amount of longhorn cheese over top.

Mix next 4 ingredients in small bowl. Add milk, cooking oil and egg. Stir until combined. Pour over beef mixture.

Sprinkle peppers and second amount of chili powder over top. Bake in 350°F (175°C) oven for 30 minutes.

Sprinkle with Monterey Jack cheese. Bake for 5 minutes until cheese is melted.

(continued on next page)

Main Dishes

Sprinkle with second amount of longhorn cheese. Bake for about 5 minutes until cheese is melted. Serves 8.

1 serving: 452 Calories; 27.4 g Total Fat; 1260 mg Sodium; 29 g Protein; 30 g Carbohydrate; 3 g Dietary Fiber

Cheese Cornbread Casserole

Tomato-flavored beef with a cheesy cornbread topping.

Lean ground beef	1 lb.	454 g
Chopped onion	1/2 cup	125 mL
Bacon slices, chopped	2	2
Chopped celery	1/2 cup	125 mL
Can of diced tomatoes	14 oz.	398 mL
Can of tomato sauce	7 1/2 oz.	213 mL
Granulated sugar	1/2 tsp.	2 mL
Salt	1/2 tsp.	2 mL
Pepper	1/4 tsp.	1 mL
CORNBREAD TOPPING		
Grated sharp Cheddar cheese	1 cup	250 mL
Yellow cornmeal	1/2 cup	125 mL
All-purpose flour	1/2 cup	125 mL
Milk	2/3 cup	150 mL
Large egg	1	1
Hard margarine (or butter), melted	2 tbsp.	30 mL
Baking powder	2 tsp.	10 mL
Salt	1/4 tsp.	1 mL
Grated sharp Cheddar cheese	1 cup	250 mL

Scramble-fry ground beef in frying pan until no longer pink. Drain.

Add onion, bacon and celery. Sauté until bacon is cooked and onion and celery are soft.

Add next 5 ingredients. Stir. Turn into ungreased 2 quart (2 L) casserole. Spread evenly.

Cornbread Topping: Combine first 8 ingredients in large bowl. Stir. Spread cornmeal mixture evenly over beef mixture. Bake, uncovered, in 425°F (220°C) oven for 20 minutes.

Sprinkle second amount of cheese over top. Bake for about 2 minutes until cheese is just melted. Serves 6.

1 serving: 466 Calories; 26.3 g Total Fat; 1152 mg Sodium; 30 g Protein; 28 g Carbohydrate; 2 g Dietary Fiber

Four-Cheese Lasagne

Nice mix of cheeses. Lovely golden brown top on this moist lasagne.

Lasagna noodles	9	9
Boiling water	12 cups	3 L
Salt	1 tbsp.	15 mL
Lean ground beef	1 lb.	454 g
Chopped celery	3/4 cup	175 mL
Chopped onion	1/2 cup	125 mL
Garlic cloves, minced (or 1/2 tsp., 2 mL, powder)	2	2
Dried sweet basil	2 tsp.	10 mL
Dried whole oregano	1 tsp.	5 mL
Salt	3/4 tsp.	4 mL
Pepper	1/2 tsp.	2 mL
Can of diced tomatoes, drained	28 oz.	796 mL
Cans of tomato sauce (7 1/2 oz., 213 mL, each)	2	2
Grated medium Cheddar cheese	2 cups	500 mL
Large egg, fork-beaten	1	1
Creamed cottage cheese	1 1/2 cups	375 mL
Grated Gouda cheese	1 cup	250 mL
Grated part-skim mozzarella cheese	1 1/2 cups	375 mL

Cook noodles in boiling water and first amount of salt in large uncovered pot or Dutch oven for 10 to 12 minutes, stirring occasionally, until tender but firm. Drain. Rinse well with cold water. Drain well.

Scramble-fry ground beef, celery, onion and garlic in large frying pan until beef is no longer pink and onion is soft. Drain.

Add next 6 ingredients. Stir. Bring to a boil. Reduce heat. Simmer, uncovered, for 30 minutes, stirring occasionally.

Stir in Cheddar cheese.

Mix egg and cottage cheese in small bowl.

(continued on next page)

Main Dishes

Spread 1/2 cup (125 mL) meat sauce in bottom of ungreased 9 × 13 inch (22 × 33 cm) pan. Assemble as follows:

1. 3 lasagna noodles
2. 1/2 of remaining meat sauce
3. 1/2 of Gouda cheese
4. 3 lasagna noodles
5. All of cottage cheese mixture
6. 3 lasagna noodles
7. Remaining meat sauce
8. Remaining Gouda cheese
9. All of mozzarella cheese

Cover with greased foil. Bake in 350°F (175°C) oven for 40 minutes. Remove foil. Heat under broiler until cheese is golden. Let stand, uncovered, for 10 minutes before cutting. Cuts into 8 pieces.

1 piece: 502 Calories; 25.9 g Total Fat; 1357 mg Sodium; 38 g Protein; 30 g Carbohydrate; 3 g Dietary Fiber

Reuben Bake

If you love corned beef, you'll enjoy this.
Try with mashed potatoes for that Old Country flavor.

Can of sauerkraut, well drained	14 oz.	398 mL
Deli corned beef, cut up	3/4 lb.	340 g
Can of diced tomatoes, drained	14 oz.	398 mL
Grated Swiss cheese	2 cups	500 mL
TOPPING		
Salad dressing (or mayonnaise)	2 tbsp.	30 mL
Ketchup	1/2 tsp.	2 mL
Fine dry bread crumbs	1/2 cup	125 mL

Layer sauerkraut, corned beef, tomatoes and cheese in ungreased 1 1/2 quart (1.5 L) casserole.

Topping: Mix salad dressing and ketchup in small bowl. Add bread crumbs. Mix until crumbly. Sprinkle over top. Bake, uncovered, in 350°F (175°C) oven for 40 minutes. Serves 4.

1 serving: 495 Calories; 29.4 g Total Fat; 1827 mg Sodium; 36 g Protein; 22 g Carbohydrate; 3 g Dietary Fiber

Beef And Cheese Angelo

Kids will love this Italian-flavored dish. Rice makes for a nice change from pasta.

Lean ground beef	2 lbs.	900 g
Medium onions, chopped	2	2
Chopped fresh mushrooms	2 cups	500 mL
Can of tomato sauce	14 oz.	398 mL
Can of diced tomatoes, with juice	14 oz.	398 mL
Long grain white rice	1 cup	250 mL
Water	2 cups	500 mL
Ground oregano	1 1/2 tsp.	7 mL
Dried sweet basil	1 1/2 tsp.	7 mL
Garlic salt	1 tsp.	5 mL
Salt	1/4 tsp.	1 mL
Pepper	1/4 tsp.	1 mL
Sour cream	1 cup	250 mL
Grated provolone (or Colby) cheese	1 cup	250 mL
Grated medium Cheddar cheese	1 cup	250 mL
Large egg	1	1
Milk	1/2 cup	125 mL
Cooking oil	1 tbsp.	15 mL
All-purpose flour	1/2 cup	125 mL
Baking powder	1 tsp.	5 mL
Salt	1/8 tsp.	0.5 mL
Grated Parmesan cheese	1/4 cup	60 mL

Scramble-fry first 3 ingredients in large pot or Dutch oven until beef is no longer pink. Drain.

Add next 9 ingredients. Simmer, uncovered, for about 20 minutes until rice is tender. Turn 1/2 of beef mixture into ungreased 9 x 13 inch (22 x 33 cm) baking dish.

Spread sour cream over beef mixture. Sprinkle with provolone and Cheddar cheeses. Spoon remaining beef mixture over top.

Beat egg in small bowl until frothy. Add next 5 ingredients. Beat until smooth. Pour over beef mixture.

Sprinkle Parmesan cheese over top. Bake in 350°F (175°C) oven for about 45 minutes until golden. Serves 8 to 10.

1 serving: 541 Calories; 27 g Total Fat; 1077 mg Sodium; 36 g Protein; 38 g Carbohydrate; 2 g Dietary Fiber

Pictured on page 108.

Cheese Tunnel Meatloaf

Flavorful meat combines so well with cheesy tunnel.

Large egg, fork-beaten	1	1
Can of stewed tomatoes, drained	14 oz.	398 mL
Medium onion, finely chopped	1	1
Quick-cooking rolled oats (not instant)	1/2 cup	125 mL
Fine dry bread crumbs	1/2 cup	125 mL
Worcestershire sauce	1 tbsp.	15 mL
Beef bouillon powder	2 tsp.	10 mL
Celery salt	1 tsp.	5 mL
Pepper	1/4 tsp.	1 mL
Lean ground beef	2 lbs.	900 g
Cheddar cheese sticks (3/4 oz., 21 g, each), see Note	4	4
Mozzarella cheese sticks (3/4 oz., 21 g, each), see Note	4	4
Ketchup	1/4 cup	60 mL

Combine first 9 ingredients in large bowl.

Add ground beef. Mix well. Cover small wire rack with foil. Place on baking sheet with sides. Place 1/3 of beef mixture on foil-covered rack. Form into 9 x 5 x 1 inch (22 x 12.5 x 2.5 cm) rectangle. Using 1/2 of remaining beef mixture, form 4 walls, 1 inch (2.5 cm) thick and 2 inches (5 cm) high, on top of rectangle.

Lay both kinds of cheese sticks in cavity. Cover with remaining beef mixture. Seal, enclosing cheese completely. Shape into oval loaf.

Spread ketchup over top and sides of loaf. Bake in 350°F (175°C) oven for about 1 3/4 hours until internal temperature registers 180°F (82°C). Let stand for 15 minutes before cutting. Serves 8.

1 serving: 424 Calories; 25.6 g Total Fat; 821 mg Sodium; 30 g Protein; 17 g Carbohydrate; 2 g Dietary Fiber

Pictured on page 125.

Note: To make your own cheese sticks, cut 3 oz. (85 g) Cheddar or mozzarella cheese into 1/2 inch (12 mm) finger-length sticks.

Cheese Steak Sandwiches

Philly Cheese Steak originated in the '30s in Philadelphia—or so the story goes. Ready in 20 minutes.

All-purpose flour	1 tsp.	5 mL
Paprika	1/2 tsp.	2 mL
Pepper	1/4 tsp.	1 mL
Garlic powder	1/8 tsp.	0.5 mL
Cayenne pepper, sprinkle		
Top sirloin steak, trimmed of fat	1 lb.	454 g
Cooking oil	1 tbsp.	15 mL
Large onion, thinly sliced	1	1
Water	2 tbsp.	30 mL
Salt	1/4 tsp.	1 mL
Grated Monterey Jack With Jalapeño cheese	3/4 cup	175 mL
Grated mozzarella cheese	3/4 cup	175 mL
Crusty French rolls, halved (toasted and buttered, optional)	6	6

Combine first 5 ingredients in small bowl. Sprinkle over both sides of steak.

Heat cooking oil on medium-high in large cast iron or heavy frying pan until very hot. Sear steak on 1 side for 2 minutes. Turn over. Sear for about 3 minutes until browned and cooked almost to desired doneness. Remove steak to cutting board. Tent with foil. Steak will continue to cook as it stands.

Add onion and water to same frying pan. Reduce heat to medium. Stir, scraping up brown bits from pan. Cook for about 10 minutes, stirring occasionally, until onion is very brown and soft. Reduce heat to low. Spread onion over bottom of frying pan.

Sprinkle salt over onion. Thinly slice steak across grain on sharp diagonal. Lay over onion. Pour any accumulated juices over steak.

Sprinkle both cheeses over steak. Cover. Cook on low for 1 to 2 minutes until cheese is melted and hot.

Divide steak mixture into 6 equal portions. Carefully lift and place on bottom halves of rolls. Cover each with top half of roll. Makes 6 sandwiches.

1 sandwich: 326 Calories; 14.7 g Total Fat; 502 mg Sodium; 25 g Protein; 22 g Carbohydrate; trace Dietary Fiber

Main Dishes

Capellini Bake

A delicious, hearty weekday casserole made with cream-style corn and salsa.

Lean ground beef	1 1/2 lbs.	680 g
Medium onion, chopped	1	1
Capellini (or angel hair) pasta	8 oz.	225 g
Boiling water	12 cups	3 L
Salt	1 tbsp.	15 mL
Jar of salsa	15 oz.	430 mL
Can of cream-style corn	14 oz.	398 mL
Grated Havarti (or Dofino) cheese	2 cups	500 mL
Salt	1/2 tsp.	2 mL
Pepper	1/8 tsp.	0.5 mL

Scramble-fry ground beef and onion in large pot or Dutch oven until beef is no longer pink and onion is soft. Drain.

Cook pasta in boiling water and salt in large uncovered pot or Dutch oven for 5 to 6 minutes until tender but firm. Drain. Add to beef mixture.

Add remaining 5 ingredients. Stir. Turn into ungreased 3 quart (3 L) casserole. Bake, uncovered, in 350°F (175°C) oven for about 30 minutes until hot and bubbly. Makes about 9 cups (2.25 L).

1 cup (250 mL): 349 Calories; 14.1 g Total Fat; 644 mg Sodium; 25 g Protein; 32 g Carbohydrate; 2 g Dietary Fiber

 To prevent mold from forming on cheese, place cheese and a few lumps of sugar in a sealable container. Another way to prevent mold formation on cheese is to dampen paper towel with white vinegar. Place in sealable container prior to adding cheese.

Chicken Tetrazzini

Mmm…comfort food. Mushroom and chicken in a nice creamy sauce.
Not too rich.

Capellini (or angel hair) pasta	8 oz.	225 g
Boiling water	12 cups	3 L
Salt	1 tbsp.	15 mL
Finely chopped celery	1/2 cup	125 mL
Medium onion, chopped	1	1
Sliced fresh mushrooms (or 10 oz., 284 mL, can, drained)	2 cups	500 mL
Hard margarine (or butter)	2 tbsp.	30 mL
Can of condensed cream of mushroom soup	10 oz.	284 mL
Can of condensed chicken broth	10 oz.	284 mL
Milk	1/2 cup	125 mL
Cubed cooked chicken (about 1 lb., 454 g, uncooked)	3 cups	750 mL
Grated medium Cheddar cheese	2 cups	500 mL
Sherry (or alcohol-free sherry)	2 tbsp.	30 mL
Finely grated Parmesan cheese	1/3 cup	75 mL

Cook pasta in boiling water and salt in large uncovered pot or Dutch oven for 4 to 6 minutes, stirring occasionally, until tender but firm. Drain. Remove to bowl. Keep warm.

Sauté celery, onion and mushrooms in margarine in same pot until onion is soft.

Add next 6 ingredients. Stir well. Remove from heat. Add pasta. Mix. Turn into ungreased 3 quart (3 L) casserole.

Sprinkle Parmesan cheese over top. Bake, uncovered, in 350°F (175°C) oven for 30 minutes until heated through and golden. Makes about 9 cups (2.25 L).

1 cup (250 mL): 375 Calories; 17.1 g Total Fat; 765 mg Sodium; 29 g Protein; 25 g Carbohydrate; 1 g Dietary Fiber

Lazy Chicken Cordon Bleu

Not as dramatic as the traditional rolled breasts. The flavor
is similar—without the effort! Very tasty. These can be individually frozen
after baking and then used for a sandwich by just heating in the microwave.

Can of condensed cream of chicken soup	10 oz.	284 mL
Milk	1/3 cup	75 mL
Boneless, skinless chicken breast halves (about 1 1/2 lbs., 680 g), pounded thin	6	6
Cooked ham slices (about 2 3/4 oz., 80 g)	6	6
Swiss cheese slices (about 3 1/2 oz., 100 g)	6	6
TOPPING		
Hard margarine (or butter)	2 tbsp.	30 mL
Fine dry bread crumbs	1/2 cup	125 mL
Grated Swiss cheese	1/3 cup	75 mL

Mix soup and milk in small bowl.

Arrange chicken 1 inch (2.5 cm) apart in greased 9 x 13 inch (22 x 33 cm) baking dish. Place 1 ham slice and 1 cheese slice over each. Spoon soup mixture over top and around chicken.

Topping: Melt margarine in small saucepan. Stir in bread crumbs and cheese until well mixed. Sprinkle over soup. Bake, uncovered, in 325°F (160°C) oven for 1 to 1 1/2 hours until bubbly, golden and chicken is no longer pink. Serves 6.

1 serving: 354 Calories; 16.4 g Total Fat; 780 mg Sodium; 38 g Protein; 12 g Carbohydrate; 1 g Dietary Fiber

Paré Pointer
If you're locked out, just sing until you get the right key.

Chicken Divan

Tender chicken with great curry flavor.
Tasty lemon, sour cream and mayonnaise sauce.

Boneless, skinless chicken breast halves (about 8)	2 lbs.	900 g
Water, to cover		
Vegetable bouillon powder	1 tbsp.	15 mL
Bag of frozen chopped broccoli	15 oz.	500 g
Water		
Can of condensed cream of chicken soup	10 oz.	284 mL
Mayonnaise	1/2 cup	125 mL
Sour cream	1/2 cup	125 mL
Lemon juice	1 1/2 tsp.	7 mL
Curry powder	1 tsp.	5 mL
Grated medium Cheddar cheese	2 cups	500 mL
TOPPING		
Hard margarine (or butter)	3 tbsp.	50 mL
Dry coarse bread crumbs	1/2 cup	125 mL
Grated Romano cheese	1/4 cup	60 mL

Cook chicken in water to cover and bouillon powder in large saucepan for about 15 minutes until tender. Drain. Cut into bite-size pieces.

Cook broccoli in water in large saucepan until tender. Drain. Scatter over bottom of greased 9 x 13 inch (22 x 33 cm) baking dish. Arrange chicken over top.

Stir next 5 ingredients together in medium bowl. Spoon over chicken.

Sprinkle with Cheddar cheese.

Topping: Melt margarine in small saucepan. Stir in bread crumbs and Romano cheese until well mixed. Sprinkle over Cheddar cheese. Bake in 350°F (175°C) oven for about 35 minutes until very hot. Serves 8.

1 serving: 512 Calories; 33.8 g Total Fat; 949 mg Sodium; 38 g Protein; 13 g Carbohydrate; 2 g Dietary Fiber

Chicken Parmesan

Moist tender chicken pieces topped with cheese and pizza sauce.

All-purpose flour	1/3 cup	75 mL
Large eggs	2	2
Fine dry bread crumbs	3/4 cup	175 mL
Salt	1 tsp.	5 mL
Pepper	1/4 tsp.	1 mL
Paprika	1/2 tsp.	2 mL
Bone-in chicken parts, skin removed	3 lbs.	1.4 kg
Cooking oil	1 tbsp.	15 mL
Medium onion, chopped	1	1
Cooking oil	2 tsp.	10 mL
Jar of pizza sauce	14 oz.	398 mL
Grated part-skim mozzarella cheese	1 1/2 cups	375 mL
Grated Parmesan cheese	1/4 cup	60 mL

Put flour into shallow dish or onto waxed paper.

Fork-beat eggs in separate shallow dish.

Combine bread crumbs, salt, pepper and paprika in separate shallow dish or on waxed paper.

Press chicken into flour to coat completely. Dip into egg. Press into bread crumb mixture to coat completely. Quickly brown both sides of chicken in first amount of cooking oil in frying pan on medium-high. Transfer to greased 9 x 13 inch (22 x 33 cm) baking dish.

Sauté onion in second amount of cooking oil in frying pan until soft.

Add pizza sauce. Stir. Pour over chicken.

Sprinkle with both cheeses. Bake, uncovered, in 350°F (175°C) oven for about 1 hour until golden and cheese is melted. Serves 4.

1 serving: 687 Calories; 29.2 g Total Fat; 1799 mg Sodium; 59 g Protein; 45 g Carbohydrate; 3 g Dietary Fiber

Pictured on page 125.

Seafood And Broccoli Mornay

Serve this fancy dish with a crisp salad and biscuits.
Try the Seafood And Couscous Mornay variation for a complete meal.

Water	1 cup	250 mL
White (or alcohol-free) wine (optional)	1/4 cup	60 mL
Bay leaf	1	1
Fresh parsley sprig	1	1
Cayenne pepper, just a pinch		
Fresh small bay scallops (or frozen, thawed)	7 oz.	200 g
Fresh medium shrimp (or frozen, thawed), peeled, deveined and tails removed	7 oz.	200 g
Mornay Sauce, page 112		
Can of crabmeat, drained and cartilage removed	4 1/4 oz.	120 g
Broccoli florets, 1 inch (2.5 cm) pieces (about 1 lb., 454 g)	3 1/2 cups	875 mL
Boiling water	1 cup	250 mL
Salt	1 tsp.	5 mL
Grated Asiago (or Swiss) cheese	1/2 cup	125 mL
Paprika, sprinkle (optional)		

Combine water, wine, bay leaf, parsley sprig and cayenne pepper in medium saucepan. Bring to a boil.

Add scallops and shrimp. Bring to a boil. Boil, uncovered, for 1 minute. Remove from heat. Let stand for 2 minutes. Drain liquid. Remove and discard bay leaf and parsley sprig.

Fold seafood mixture into Mornay Sauce in large bowl. Add crab. Stir. Set aside.

Simmer broccoli in boiling water and salt in large saucepan for about 2 minutes until bright green and barely tender-crisp. Drain. Rinse with cold water. Drain well. Arrange broccoli in 4 ungreased individual ovenproof serving dishes. Spoon seafood mixture over broccoli.

(continued on next page)

Main Dishes

Sprinkle Asiago cheese and paprika over each serving. Bake, uncovered, in 350°F (175°C) oven for about 30 minutes until bubbly and cheese is golden. Serves 4.

1 serving: 259 Calories; 10.3 g Total Fat; 521 mg Sodium; 32 g Protein; 9 g Carbohydrate; 2 g Dietary Fiber

Pictured on page 125.

SEAFOOD AND ASPARAGUS MORNAY: Omit broccoli. Use about 1 lb. (454 g) asparagus, cut into 1 inch (2.5 cm) pieces.

SEAFOOD AND PEA PODS MORNAY: Omit broccoli. Use about 1 lb. (454 g) pea pods.

SEAFOOD AND COUSCOUS MORNAY: Scatter about 1/3 cup (75 mL) prepared couscous in bottom of each serving dish before adding broccoli.

Cheesy Fish Fillets

Oven-baked fish broiled briefly for a very attractive and tasty dish.

Cod fillets	1 lb.	454 g
Light sour cream	1/4 cup	60 mL
Lemon juice	1 tbsp.	15 mL
Garlic salt	1/2 tsp.	2 mL
Dill weed	1/2 tsp.	2 mL
Grated Havarti (or Dofino) cheese	1/3 cup	75 mL

Arrange fillets in single layer on greased baking sheet with sides.

Combine sour cream, lemon juice, garlic salt and dill weed in small bowl. Spoon over fillets.

Sprinkle with cheese. Bake, uncovered, in 350°F (175°C) oven for 12 to 14 minutes until fish flakes easily when tested with fork. Broil for 2 to 3 minutes until cheese is bubbly and golden. Do not allow tops to brown too much. Serves 4.

1 serving: 144 Calories; 4.4 g Total Fat; 241 mg Sodium; 23 g Protein; 2 g Carbohydrate; trace Dietary Fiber

Pictured on page 108.

Macaroni With Eggs

Macaroni and cheese with a twist!

Elbow macaroni	2 cups	500 mL
Boiling water	10 cups	2.5 L
Salt	2 tsp.	10 mL
Large eggs	2	2
Milk	2 1/2 cups	625 mL
Onion powder	1 tsp.	5 mL
Paprika	1/2 tsp.	2 mL
Salt	1 tsp.	5 mL
Pepper	1/2 tsp.	2 mL
Grated extra sharp Cheddar cheese	1 cup	250 mL

Cook macaroni in boiling water and salt in large uncovered pot or Dutch oven for 5 to 7 minutes, stirring occasionally, until tender but firm. Drain. Turn into ungreased 3 quart (3 L) casserole.

Beat eggs in medium bowl until frothy. Add milk, onion powder, paprika, salt and pepper. Beat on low until mixed.

Add cheese. Stir. Pour over macaroni. Stir gently. Bake, uncovered, in 350°F (175°C) oven for about 40 minutes until set. Serves 6.

1 serving: 289 Calories; 10 g Total Fat; 597 mg Sodium; 15 g Protein; 34 g Carbohydrate; 1 g Dietary Fiber

1. Cheese-Stuffed Portobello Mushrooms, page 110
2. Cheese And Bean Cassoulet, page 116
3. Stuffed-Crust Pizza, page 114

Props Courtesy Of: Anchor Hocking Canada

Shelf Pasta

When time is short, this fills the need. Good flavor. Doubles easily.

Package of macaroni and cheese dinner	7 3/4 oz.	220 g
Chopped green onion	2 tbsp.	30 mL
White bread slice, cubed	1	1
Hard margarine (or butter)	2 tbsp.	30 mL
Creamed cottage cheese	1 cup	250 mL
Seasoned salt	1/2 tsp.	2 mL

Prepare macaroni and cheese dinner according to package directions.

Sauté green onion and bread cubes in margarine in frying pan until green onion is soft.

Add cottage cheese and seasoned salt to macaroni and cheese. Stir until heated through. Turn into serving bowl. Place onion mixture over macaroni mixture. Makes 3 1/2 cups (875 mL).

1 cup (250 mL): 459 Calories; 20.5 g Total Fat; 1851 mg Sodium; 19 g Protein; 9 g Carbohydrate; 1 g Dietary Fiber

Pictured on page 90.

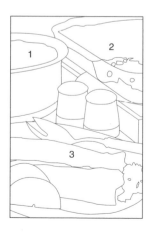

1. Egg And Onion Casserole, page 111
2. Beef And Cheese Angelo, page 96
3. Cheesy Fish Fillets, page 105

Props Courtesy Of: Pyrex Originals
The Bay

Cheese-Stuffed Portobello Mushrooms

This is a tasty, meatless main course that can also be served as a starter appetizer.

Finely chopped onion	1/2 cup	125 mL
Garlic clove, minced (or 1/4 tsp., 1 mL, powder)	1	1
Olive (or cooking) oil	2 tsp.	10 mL
Fresh spinach leaves (about 2 cups, 500 mL, packed)	2 oz.	57 g
Finely chopped oil-packed sun-dried tomatoes, drained	1/4 cup	60 mL
Chopped fresh sweet basil (or 1/2 tsp., 2 mL, dried)	2 tsp.	10 mL
Chopped fresh oregano leaves (or 1/4 tsp., 1 mL, dried)	1 tsp.	5 mL
Pepper, sprinkle		
Caesar-flavored croutons, slightly crushed if very large	1 cup	250 mL
Feta cheese (about 5 oz., 140 g), crumbled (see Note)	1 cup	250 mL
Medium portobello mushrooms (about 4 – 5 inches, 10 – 12.5 cm, in diameter)	6	6

Sauté onion and garlic in olive oil in frying pan until onion is soft.

Stack several spinach leaves. Roll tightly lengthwise. Cut crosswise into thin strands. Add to onion mixture. Sauté for 2 to 3 minutes until spinach is just wilted. Remove from heat.

Add tomato, basil, oregano, pepper and croutons. Stir. Cool slightly.

Stir in cheese.

Remove and discard stems of mushrooms. Scrape or cut out and discard black "gills" from underside of mushrooms. Spoon 1/3 to 1/2 cup (75 to 125 mL) filling into each mushroom cap. Pack slightly. Arrange in single layer in ungreased 9 x 13 inch (22 x 33 cm) baking dish. Cover with foil. Bake in 375°F (190°C) oven for 30 minutes until mushrooms are soft. Makes 6 stuffed mushrooms.

1 stuffed mushroom: 155 Calories; 9.1 g Total Fat; 454 mg Sodium; 7 g Protein; 13 g Carbohydrate; 2 g Dietary Fiber

Pictured on page 107.

Note: A flavored feta cheese, such as basil tomato or herb, can be used for even more flavor.

Main Dishes

Egg And Onion Casserole

*Cheesy and creamy are both accurate descriptions for
this mild onion-flavored casserole.*

Hard margarine (or butter)	1/3 cup	75 mL
All-purpose flour	1/3 cup	75 mL
Prepared mustard	1 tbsp.	15 mL
Salt	3/4 tsp.	4 mL
Pepper	1/4 tsp.	1 mL
Milk	3 cups	750 mL
Gruyère cheese, diced (about 2 cups, 500 mL)	1/2 lb.	225 g
Thinly sliced sweet onion (such as Vidalia or Walla Walla)	6 cups	1.5 L
Hard margarine (or butter)	1/3 cup	75 mL
Thinly sliced fresh mushrooms	2 cups	500 mL
Hard-boiled eggs, sliced	12	12
Paprika, sprinkle		

Melt first amount of margarine in medium saucepan. Mix in flour, mustard, salt and pepper until smooth. Stir in milk until boiling and thickened.

Add cheese. Stir until melted. Do not boil. Remove from heat. Set aside.

Sauté onion in second amount of margarine in large frying pan for about 10 minutes until soft and clear. Turn into ungreased 2 quart (2 L) casserole.

Place mushrooms in same frying pan. Sauté on medium-high for about 5 minutes until liquid from mushrooms has evaporated. Layer over onions. Pour about 1 cup (250 mL) cheese mixture over mushrooms. Stir gently.

Layer egg slices over cheese mixture. Spoon remaining cheese mixture over all.

Sprinkle with paprika. Bake, uncovered, in 350°F (175°C) oven for about 20 minutes until golden. Serves 6 to 8.

1 serving: 654 Calories; 46.1 g Total Fat; 903 mg Sodium; 32 g Protein; 29 g Carbohydrate; 3 g Dietary Fiber

Pictured on page 108.

Mornay Sauce

This sauce is delicious as the base for any baked vegetable dishes and especially Seafood And Broccoli Mornay, page 104. It's also very good spooned over eggs on toast to fancy them up a bit. Can be chilled or frozen and reheated with no alteration in texture. A great make-ahead recipe.

Finely chopped onion	2 tbsp.	30 mL
Finely chopped garlic (optional)	1/4 tsp.	1 mL
Hard margarine (or butter)	3 tbsp.	50 mL
All-purpose flour	2 tbsp.	30 mL
Milk	1 1/3 cups	325 mL
Egg yolk (large)	1	1
Half-and-half cream (or homogenized milk)	1/4 cup	60 mL
Salt	1/4 tsp.	1 mL
Cayenne pepper	1/16 tsp.	0.5 mL
Grated Asiago (or Swiss) cheese	1/2 cup	125 mL

Sauté onion and garlic in margarine in medium saucepan until onion is soft.

Sprinkle flour over onion mixture. Stir on low for 1 minute until combined. Increase heat to medium. Gradually stir in milk until boiling and thickened.

Fork-beat egg yolk and cream together in small dish. Add large spoonful of hot milk mixture to egg mixture. Stir until egg yolk mixture is warm. Add to milk mixture. Heat and stir for 3 to 4 minutes until creamy and thickened.

Add salt, cayenne pepper and cheese. Heat and stir until cheese is melted. Makes 1 3/4 cups (425 mL).

2 tbsp. (30 mL): 61 Calories; 4.7 g Total Fat; 96 mg Sodium; 2 g Protein; 3 g Carbohydrate; trace Dietary Fiber

Pictured on page 125.

Pictured on page 125.

Paré Pointer

When your food tastes like soap, you know the cafeteria's kitchen is clean.

Plain Cheese Pizza

A whole wheat crust encases three quarters of a pound of flavorful and stringy cheese. Kids will definitely like this one—nothing to pick off!

CRUST

Very warm water	1 cup	250 mL
Granulated sugar	1 tsp.	5 mL
Olive (or cooking) oil	1 tbsp.	15 mL
Salt	1 tsp.	5 mL
All-purpose flour	1 cup	250 mL
Instant yeast (or 1/4 oz., 8 g, envelope)	2 1/4 tsp.	11 mL
Whole wheat flour, approximately	1 1/3 cups	325 mL

TOPPINGS

Pizza sauce	1/2 cup	125 mL
Chopped fresh sweet basil (or 3/4 tsp., 4 mL, dried), optional	1 tbsp.	15 mL
Freshly grated Parmesan cheese	3 tbsp.	50 mL
Grated mozzarella cheese	1 1/2 cups	375 mL
Grated Asiago cheese	1 1/2 cups	375 mL

Crust: Mix first 4 ingredients in medium bowl until sugar is dissolved.

Combine all-purpose flour and yeast in small bowl. Stir into water mixture until smooth.

Work in enough whole wheat flour until dough is no longer sticky. Turn out onto lightly floured surface. Knead for 2 minutes. Cover. Let stand for 15 minutes. Roll out and press in greased 12 inch (30 cm) pizza pan, forming small rim around edge.

Toppings: Spread pizza sauce on dough to edge. Sprinkle with basil and Parmesan cheese. Let stand, uncovered, in oven with light on and door closed for 30 minutes until doubled in size.

Sprinkle both cheeses over top. Bake on center rack in 450°F (230°C) oven for 13 to 15 minutes until cheese is melted and crust is browned. Cuts into 8 wedges.

1 wedge: 327 Calories; 14.7 g Total Fat; 567 mg Sodium; 17 g Protein; 33 g Carbohydrate; 4 g Dietary Fiber

Stuffed-Crust Pizza

A puffy cheese-filled crust will make this a favorite.
A bit different with pesto instead of pizza sauce. Delightful!

CHEESE-STUFFED CRUST

Very warm water	1 1/4 cups	300 mL
Granulated sugar	1 tsp.	5 mL
Olive (or cooking) oil	1 tbsp.	15 mL
Salt	1 tsp.	5 mL
All-purpose flour, approximately	1 1/2 cups	375 mL
Instant yeast (or 1/4 oz., 8 g, envelope)	2 1/4 tsp.	11 mL
Flaxseed	2 tsp.	10 mL
All-purpose flour	1 1/2 cups	375 mL
Mozzarella cheese sticks (3/4 oz., 21 g, each), see Note	7	7

TOPPINGS

Basil (or sun-dried tomato) pesto	3 tbsp.	50 mL
Diced cooked chicken (or lean ham)	1 cup	250 mL
Grated mozzarella cheese	1 1/2 cups	375 mL
Roasted red pepper (or 1/2 of 14 oz., 398 mL, can, drained), cut into strips	1	1
Thinly sliced red onion rings	1/2 cup	125 mL
Freshly grated Romano cheese	3 tbsp.	50 mL
Fresh tomato slices (about 1 large)	8	8

Cheese-Stuffed Crust: Stir first 4 ingredients together in medium bowl until sugar is dissolved.

Combine first amount of flour and yeast in small bowl. Stir into water mixture until smooth.

Work in flaxseed and enough of second amount of flour until dough is no longer sticky. Turn out onto lightly floured surface. Knead for 2 minutes. Cover. Let stand for 15 minutes. Roll out into 13 inch (33 cm) circle and press in greased 12 inch (30 cm) pizza pan, letting excess dough drape over edge.

Roll up cheese sticks in excess dough all around edge. Pinch edge to base of crust to seal.

(continued on next page)

Toppings: Spread pesto on crust just to beginning of rolled crust. Cover with waxed paper. Let stand in oven with light on and door closed for 30 minutes until doubled in size.

Layer next 5 ingredients on crust in order given. Bake on center rack in 450°F (230°C) oven for 15 to 20 minutes until cheese is melted and crust is browned.

Arrange tomato slices on top. Cuts into 8 wedges.

1 wedge: 386 Calories; 13.8 g Total Fat; 505 mg Sodium; 21 g Protein; 44 g Carbohydrate; 3 g Dietary Fiber

Pictured on page 107.

Note: To make cheese sticks, cut 5 oz. (140 g) mozzarella cheese into 1/2 inch (12 mm) finger-length sticks.

Ham And Gruyère Casserole

Cheesy cream sauce with a tasty crumb topping.

Medium onion, chopped	1	1
Hard margarine (or butter)	1 tbsp.	15 mL
Sliced fresh mushrooms	2 cups	500 mL
Milk	1 1/2 cups	375 mL
All-purpose flour	1/4 cup	60 mL
Pepper	1/4 tsp.	1 mL
Grated Gruyère cheese	1 cup	250 mL
Bite-size pieces of cooked ham	2 cups	500 mL
Sherry (or alcohol-free sherry)	2 tbsp.	30 mL
Hard margarine (or butter)	1 tbsp.	15 mL
Fine dry bread crumbs	1/3 cup	75 mL

Sauté onion in first amount of margarine in frying pan until soft.

Add mushrooms. Sauté until golden.

Stir milk into flour and pepper in small bowl until smooth. Gradually stir into onion mixture until boiling and thickened.

Add cheese, ham and sherry. Stir until cheese starts to melt. Turn into greased 1 1/2 quart (1.5 L) casserole.

Melt second amount of margarine in small saucepan. Add bread crumbs. Stir well. Sprinkle over ham mixture. Bake, uncovered, in 350°F (175°C) oven for about 30 minutes until hot and golden. Serves 4 to 6.

1 serving: 485 Calories; 27.7 g Total Fat; 1290 mg Sodium; 33 g Protein; 24 g Carbohydrate; 2 g Dietary Fiber

Cheese And Bean Cassoulet

Chunks of sausage with green beans and kidney beans in a cheesy sauce.

Chopped onion	1/2 cup	125 mL
Chopped celery	1/2 cup	125 mL
Hard margarine (or butter)	1 tbsp.	15 mL
Smoked farmers' sausage, sliced 1/4 inch (6 mm) thick	1 lb.	454 g
Cans of white kidney beans (19 oz., 540 mL, each), drained and rinsed	2	2
Prepared chicken broth	1/2 cup	125 mL
Poultry seasoning	1 tsp.	5 mL
Can of diced tomatoes, drained	14 oz.	398 mL
Frozen cut green beans	2 cups	500 mL
Pasteurized cheese loaf, cubed (such as Velveeta)	9 oz.	250 g
Hard margarine (or butter)	1 tbsp.	15 mL
Fine dry bread crumbs	1/2 cup	125 mL
Chopped fresh parsley (or 1 tbsp., 15 mL, flakes)	1/4 cup	60 mL

Sauté onion and celery in first amount of margarine in large pot or Dutch oven until soft.

Add sausage. Heat for 5 minutes, stirring occasionally.

Add next 5 ingredients. Bring to a boil. Reduce heat to medium-low. Cover. Simmer for 5 minutes.

Add cheese. Stir until melted. Spoon into ungreased 2 quart (2 L) casserole.

Combine second amount of margarine, bread crumbs and parsley in small frying pan. Heat and stir until bread crumbs are lightly browned. Sprinkle over cheese mixture. Makes 8 cups (2 L).

1 cup (250 mL): 468 Calories; 30.5 g Total Fat; 1100 mg Sodium; 23 g Protein; 27 g Carbohydrate; 1 g Dietary Fiber

Pictured on page 107.

Baked Radiatore Alfredo

*Use individual baking dishes for presentation of this rich and
oh so decadent dish. Very definite flavor of Asiago cheese.*

Radiatore pasta	12 oz.	340 g
Boiling water	16 cups	4 L
Salt	4 tsp.	20 mL
Alfredo White Sauce, page 121	2/3 cup	150 mL
Grated Asiago cheese	1 cup	250 mL
Grated part-skim mozzarella cheese	1 cup	250 mL
Finely grated Parmesan (or Romano) cheese	2 tbsp.	30 mL
Paprika	1/2 tsp.	2 mL
Freshly chopped parsley (or 1/2 tsp., 2 mL, flakes)	2 tsp.	10 mL

Cook pasta in boiling water and salt in large uncovered pot or Dutch oven
for 10 to 12 minutes, stirring occasionally, until tender but firm. Drain.
Rinse with cold water. Drain well.

Divide pasta among 4 lightly greased individual serving size casseroles.
Spoon Alfredo White Sauce over pasta.

Toss all 3 cheeses together in small bowl. Divide and sprinkle over each
serving.

Divide and sprinkle paprika and parsley over each serving. Bake,
uncovered, on center rack in 400°F (205°C) oven for 15 to 20 minutes
until bubbly and golden. Serves 4.

*1 serving: 649 Calories; 25.4 g Total Fat; 463 mg Sodium; 35 g Protein; 68 g Carbohydrate;
2 g Dietary Fiber*

Pictured on front cover.

 *To freeze cheese, wrap tightly in foil or thick plastic. Double wrapping
and making it as airtight as possible help prevent moisture loss, which
is the main contributor to a change in texture.*

Three-Cheese Manicotti

Very cheesy and very rich! Spicy and sweet.

Manicotti pasta shells	8	8
Boiling water	12 cups	3 L
Salt	2 tsp.	10 mL
CHEESE FILLING		
Dry curd cottage cheese, pushed through sieve or put through food mill until very finely textured	2 cups	500 mL
Grated mozzarella cheese	2 cups	500 mL
Finely grated Romano cheese	3/4 cup	175 mL
Chopped fresh parsley (or 2 1/2 tsp., 12 mL, flakes)	3 tbsp.	50 mL
Finely chopped fresh chives (or 2 1/2 tsp., 12 mL, dried)	3 tbsp.	50 mL
Large eggs, fork-beaten	2	2
Salt	1/2 tsp.	2 mL
SPICED MEAT SAUCE		
Extra lean ground beef	1/2 lb.	225 g
Chopped onion	1 cup	250 mL
Garlic cloves, minced (or 1/2 tsp., 2 mL, powder), optional	2	2
Olive (or cooking) oil	1 tbsp.	15 mL
Can of tomato sauce	14 oz.	398 mL
Can of whole roma (plum) tomatoes, with juice, mashed	14 oz.	398 mL
Sweet chili sauce	1/4 cup	60 mL
Brown sugar, packed	1 tsp.	5 mL
Hot pepper sauce	1/2 tsp.	2 mL
Chopped fresh sweet basil (or 1 tsp., 5 mL, dried)	1 1/2 tbsp.	25 mL
Chopped fresh marjoram leaves (or 3/4 tsp., 4 mL, dried)	1 tbsp.	15 mL
Grated mozzarella cheese	1 cup	250 mL
Finely grated Romano cheese	1/4 cup	60 mL

Cook pasta in boiling water and salt in large uncovered pot or Dutch oven for 5 to 6 minutes, stirring occasionally, until tender but firm. Drain. Rinse under cold water. Drain well.

(continued on next page)

Main Dishes

Cheese Filling: Combine all 7 ingredients in medium bowl. Makes 3 cups (750 mL) filling. Spoon about 1/3 cup (75 mL) filling into each shell. Don't overfill to prevent splitting. Arrange in single layer in greased 9 x 13 inch (22 x 33 cm) pan. Set aside.

Spiced Meat Sauce: Scramble-fry ground beef, onion and garlic in olive oil in large frying pan until beef is no longer pink. Drain.

Add next 5 ingredients. Bring to a boil. Reduce heat. Simmer, uncovered, for 20 minutes until slightly thickened.

Add basil and marjoram. Stir. Pour over pasta.

Sprinkle with mozzarella and Romano cheeses. Bake, uncovered, in 350°F (175°C) oven for about 30 minutes until bubbly and cheese has melted. Serves 4 to 6.

1 serving: 798 Calories; 42.5 g Total Fat; 2095 mg Sodium; 63 g Protein; 41 g Carbohydrate; 5 g Dietary Fiber

Pictured on page 90.

Vermicelli Plate With Myzithra

Different but good! Pale-colored pasta with bits of white cheese throughout.

Vermicelli	8 oz.	225 g
Boiling water	12 cups	3 L
Salt	1 tbsp.	15 mL
Butter (not margarine)	1/2 cup	125 mL
Garlic clove, halved (or 1/8 tsp., 0.5 mL, powder)	1	1
Grated Greek Myzithra cheese (about 1 cup, 250 mL)	4 oz.	113 g
Chopped fresh cilantro (or parsley)	1/3 cup	75 mL

Cook vermicelli in boiling water and salt in large uncovered pot or Dutch oven for 6 to 8 minutes until tender but firm. Drain. Keep warm.

Heat butter in medium frying pan on medium until starting to turn golden. Add garlic. Cook until butter browns. Remove and discard garlic. Pour butter over vermicelli.

Add cheese and cilantro. Toss until vermicelli is shiny. Serve immediately. Serves 4.

1 serving: 535 Calories; 34 g Total Fat; 712 mg Sodium; 13 g Protein; 44 g Carbohydrate; 1 g Dietary Fiber

Pictured on page 90.

Mushroom Wine Sauce

Creamy yellow sauce flavored with mushrooms, Swiss cheese,
parsley and thyme. Great served over pasta or vegetables.

Diced brown mushrooms	1 cup	250 mL
Finely chopped onion	1 tbsp.	15 mL
Garlic clove, minced (or 1/4 tsp., 1 mL, powder)	1	1
Hard margarine (or butter)	3 tbsp.	50 mL
Dry white (or alcohol-free) wine	1/4 cup	60 mL
Beef bouillon powder	1/2 tsp.	2 mL
Freshly ground pepper, sprinkle		
All-purpose flour	1 tbsp.	15 mL
Half-and-half cream (or homogenized milk)	2 cups	500 mL
Grated mild Cheddar cheese	1 cup	250 mL
Swiss cheese slices (about 6 oz., 170 g), torn up	8	8
Chopped fresh parsley (or 1/2 tsp., 2 mL, flakes)	2 tsp.	10 mL
Chopped fresh thyme leaves (or 1/2 tsp., 2 mL, dried)	2 tsp.	10 mL

Sauté mushrooms, onion and garlic in margarine in large saucepan until mushrooms are golden.

Stir in wine, bouillon powder and pepper. Boil until wine is reduced and absorbed into mushrooms.

Sprinkle flour over mushroom mixture. Stir for 30 to 60 seconds until well mixed. Add cream. Heat and stir on medium until boiling and very slightly thickened.

Add Cheddar and Swiss cheeses. Stir until melted.

Add parsley and thyme. Stir. Makes 2 3/4 cups (675 mL).

1/4 cup (60 mL): 155 Calories; 11.8 g Total Fat; 352 mg Sodium; 8 g Protein; 4 g Carbohydrate; trace Dietary Fiber

Alfredo White Sauce

Alfredo sauces are always very high in fat! Only indulge very occasionally and with smaller portions. The flavor is best with all three cheeses. Use for Baked Radiatore Alfredo, page 117.

Hard margarine (or butter)	1/4 cup	60 mL
All-purpose flour	1 tbsp.	15 mL
Pepper (white is best)	1/8 tsp.	0.5 mL
Half-and-half cream (or homogenized milk)	2 cups	500 mL
Grated Asiago cheese	1 1/2 cups	375 mL
Grated mozzarella cheese	1 1/2 cups	375 mL
Finely grated Parmesan (or Romano) cheese	1/2 cup	125 mL

Melt margarine in medium saucepan. Add flour and pepper. Heat and stir for 30 seconds.

Gradually stir in cream until boiling and slightly thickened. Sauce should just barely coat back of spoon. Remove from heat.

Add all 3 cheeses. Stir until melted. Makes 2 3/4 cups (675 mL).

1/4 cup (60 mL): 191 Calories; 14.8 g Total Fat; 257 mg Sodium; 11 g Protein; 4 g Carbohydrate; trace Dietary Fiber

 Cheeses such as cottage cheese, ricotta and cream cheese must be discarded immediately at the first sign of mold. These cheeses are more susceptible to a type of mold which produces a harmful toxin.

Parma Rosa Sauce

A wee bite of pepper in this wonderful combination of ingredients.
Delicious on pasta, of course, but try it with grilled peppers, zucchini,
eggplant or Bacon Cheese Strata, page 33, for a pleasant surprise.

Finely chopped onion	3/4 cup	175 mL
Fresh hot chili peppers, seeded and diced	2 - 3	2 - 3
Garlic cloves, minced (or 1/2 tsp., 2 mL, powder)	2	2
Hard margarine (or butter)	1 tbsp.	15 mL
Can of crushed tomatoes	14 oz.	398 mL
Granulated sugar	1 tsp.	5 mL
Freshly ground pepper	1/4 tsp.	1 mL
Freshly chopped sweet basil (or 1 1/2 tsp., 7 mL, dried)	2 tbsp.	30 mL
Freshly chopped oregano leaves (or 1 1/2 tsp., 7 mL, dried)	2 tbsp.	30 mL
Whipping cream	1 cup	250 mL
All-purpose flour	2 tsp.	10 mL
Freshly grated Parmesan cheese	3/4 cup	175 mL

Sauté onion, peppers and garlic in margarine in frying pan for about 4 minutes until onion is soft.

Add next 5 ingredients. Bring to a boil. Reduce heat. Simmer, uncovered, for 10 minutes, stirring occasionally.

Stir whipping cream into flour in small bowl until smooth. Gradually stir into tomato sauce until boiling and thickened.

Stir in Parmesan cheese. Makes 3 cups (750 mL).

1/4 cup (60 mL): 116 Calories; 9.4 g Total Fat; 190 mg Sodium; 4 g Protein; 5 g Carbohydrate; 1 g Dietary Fiber

LIGHT PARMA ROSA SAUCE: Omit whipping cream. Use same amount of skim evaporated milk. Use grated light Parmesan cheese in place of regular Parmesan cheese.

Ham And Cheese Pasta Salad

Crunchy and light-tasting. Easy to prepare for your next buffet, potluck or picnic.

Elbow macaroni (or gemelli pasta), about 8 oz. (225 g)	2 cups	500 mL
Boiling water	10 cups	2.5 L
Salt	2 tsp.	10 mL
Diced medium Cheddar cheese	1 cup	250 mL
Diced ham (or 6 1/2 oz., 184 g, can of flaked ham, drained)	1 cup	250 mL
Chopped celery	1/2 cup	125 mL
Green onions, chopped	3	3
DRESSING		
Salad dressing (or mayonnaise)	1/2 cup	125 mL
Sweet pickle relish	2 tbsp.	30 mL
Jar of sliced pimientos, drained	2 oz.	57 mL
Milk	2 tbsp.	30 mL
Salt	1/2 tsp.	2 mL
Pepper	1/4 tsp.	1 mL
TOPPING		
Radishes, thinly sliced	4	4
Grated medium Cheddar cheese	1/4 cup	60 mL
Salad dressing (or mayonnaise)	1 tbsp.	15 mL
Milk	1 tbsp.	15 mL

Paprika, sprinkle

Cook macaroni in boiling water and salt in large uncovered pot or Dutch oven for 5 to 7 minutes, stirring occasionally, until tender but firm. Drain. Rinse with cold water. Drain well. Turn into large salad bowl.

Add cheese, ham, celery and green onion. Toss.

Dressing: Combine all 6 ingredients in small bowl. Makes 3/4 cup (175 mL) dressing. Add to macaroni mixture. Toss until well coated. Smooth top.

Topping: Scatter radish over salad. Sprinkle cheese over top.

Combine salad dressing and milk in small cup until smooth. Drizzle over cheese.

Sprinkle paprika over all. Makes 6 cups (1.5 L). Serves 8.

1 serving: 320 Calories; 18 g Total Fat; 675 mg Sodium; 13 g Protein; 26 g Carbohydrate; 1 g Dietary Fiber

Pictured on page 126.

Tomato Cheese Salad

Red and white summery salad. Can be eaten right away
but tastes even better when left to marinate.

Diced mozzarella cheese (1/4 inch, 6 mm, dice)	2 cups	500 mL
Cubed tomato (1/2 inch, 12 mm, cubes)	3 cups	750 mL
DRESSING		
Olive (or cooking) oil	2 tbsp.	30 mL
Dried sweet basil	1 tsp.	5 mL
Onion powder	1/4 tsp.	1 mL
Parsley flakes	1/2 tsp.	2 mL
Salt	1/2 tsp.	2 mL
Pepper	1/8 tsp.	0.5 mL

Gently toss cheese and tomato together in large bowl.

Dressing: Combine all 6 ingredients in small bowl. Pour over tomato mixture. Toss until coated. Let marinate at room temperature for at least 1 hour. Makes 3 1/2 cups (875 mL).

1/2 cup (125 mL): 165 Calories; 13.1 g Total Fat; 330 mg Sodium; 9 g Protein; 4 g Carbohydrate; 1 g Dietary Fiber

Pictured on page 126.

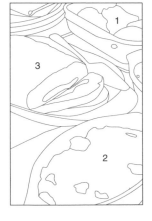

1. Chicken Parmesan, page 103
2. Seafood And Broccoli Mornay, page 104
3. Cheese Tunnel Meatloaf, page 97

Props Courtesy Of: Anchor Hocking Canada
The Bay

Cheddar Cheese Dressing

Make this at least 24 hours in advance. Will keep for at least one week in the refrigerator. The flavor gets better with time. Very complementary to dark leafy vegetables and the more bitter-type greens such as kale and endive.

Brown sugar, packed	3 tbsp.	50 mL
Salt	1 tsp.	5 mL
Dry mustard	1 tsp.	5 mL
Freshly ground pepper	1/2 tsp.	2 mL
Cooking oil	1/2 cup	125 mL
Apple cider vinegar	1/4 cup	60 mL
Tomato juice	1/4 cup	60 mL
Garlic clove, minced (or 1/4 tsp., 1 mL, powder), optional	1	1
Grated onion	1/2 tsp.	2 mL
Green onion, thinly sliced	1	1
Grated sharp Cheddar cheese, lightly packed	1 cup	250 mL

Put all 11 ingredients into 2 cup (500 mL) glass jar with tight-fitting lid. Shake vigorously until combined. May be stored in refrigerator for up to 1 week. Shake well before using. Makes 1 1/2 cups (375 mL).

2 tbsp. (30 mL): 136 Calories; 12.5 g Total Fat; 269 mg Sodium; 3 g Protein; 4 g Carbohydrate; trace Dietary Fiber

1. Tomato Cheese Salad, page 124
2. Ham And Cheese Pasta Salad, page 123
3. Jellied Fruit And Cheese Salad, page 130
4. Flaxseed Cheese Sticks, page 26

Props Courtesy Of: Anchor Hocking Canada

Light Blue Cheese Dressing

Thick dressing with mild blue cheese chunks.

Light salad dressing (such as Miracle Whip)	1/2 cup	125 mL
Light mayonnaise	1/2 cup	125 mL
Light sour cream	1/2 cup	125 mL
White vinegar	1 1/2 tsp.	7 mL
Seasoned salt	1/4 tsp.	1 mL
Garlic powder	1/8 tsp.	0.5 mL
Crumbled blue cheese (about 2 oz., 57 g)	1/2 cup	125 mL

Combine all 7 ingredients in medium bowl. May be stored in refrigerator for up to 1 week. Makes 1 3/4 cups (425 mL).

2 tbsp. (30 mL): 76 Calories; 6.8 g Total Fat; 216 mg Sodium; 1 g Protein; 3 g Carbohydrate; 0 g Dietary Fiber

Orange Delight

Orange, pineapple and cheese harmonize nicely.

Package of orange-flavored gelatin (jelly powder)	3 oz.	85 g
Boiling water	1 cup	250 mL
Can of crushed pineapple, drained	14 oz.	398 mL
Light sour cream	1 cup	250 mL
Can of mandarin orange segments, drained	10 oz.	284 mL
Grated medium Cheddar cheese	1 cup	250 mL

Stir jelly powder into boiling water in medium bowl until dissolved.

Add pineapple, sour cream and orange segments. Stir. Chill for about 1 hour, stirring and scraping down sides of bowl occasionally, until syrupy.

Fold in cheese. Pour into greased 6 cup (1.5 L) mold or deep bowl. Chill until set. Invert salad onto dampened serving plate. Dampness makes it easier to center mold on plate. Serves 8.

1 serving: 153 Calories; 7.2 g Total Fat; 133 mg Sodium; 6 g Protein; 18 g Carbohydrate; 1 g Dietary Fiber

Salads

Layered Lime Individual Salads

Crunchy, green salad. Prepare molds a day or two ahead.

Package of lime-flavored gelatin (jelly powder)	3 oz.	85 g
Boiling water	3/4 cup	175 mL
Pineapple juice	1 1/4 cups	300 mL
Lemon juice	1/2 tsp.	2 mL
Salt	1/4 tsp.	1 mL
Package of lime-flavored gelatin (jelly powder)	3 oz.	85 g
Boiling water	3/4 cup	175 mL
Onion powder	1/8 tsp.	0.5 mL
Salt	1/4 tsp.	1 mL
Creamed cottage cheese, sieved or processed in blender until smooth	1 1/2 cups	375 mL
Finely chopped celery	1/2 cup	125 mL
Peeled, seeded and grated English cucumber, squeezed dry	1/2 cup	125 mL
Chopped chives	1 tsp.	5 mL
Lemon juice	1/2 tsp.	2 mL
Lettuce leaves	8	8
Salad dressing (or mayonnaise)	4 tsp.	20 mL

Dissolve first amount of jelly powder in first amount of boiling water in small bowl. Add pineapple juice, lemon juice and first amount of salt. Stir. Pour 2 tbsp. (30 mL) into each of 8 greased individual salad molds or small deep bowls. Chill until firm. Reserve remaining jelly mixture.

Dissolve second amount of jelly powder in second amount of boiling water in separate small bowl. Add onion powder and second amount of salt. Stir. Add reserved jelly mixture. Stir.

Add next 5 ingredients. Stir. Chill for about 1 1/2 hours, stirring and scraping down sides of bowl occasionally, until syrupy. Spoon over firm jelly mixture. Chill until set.

Invert each salad onto 1 lettuce leaf on small plate. Top each salad with 1/2 tsp. (2 mL) salad dressing. Serves 8.

1 serving: 164 Calories; 3.2 g Total Fat; 395 mg Sodium; 7 g Protein; 27 g Carbohydrate; trace Dietary Fiber

Jellied Fruit And Cheese Salad

Bright green, fruity gelatin with cream cheese topping.
Very pretty to serve at a meeting or luncheon.
Lower in fat with light cream cheese and light mayonnaise.

Packages of lime-flavored gelatin (jelly powder), 3 oz. (85 g) each	2	2
Boiling water	2 cups	500 mL
Reserved pear juice, plus water to make	2 cups	500 mL
Can of pears, drained, juice reserved and pears diced	14 oz.	398 mL
Medium bananas, sliced	2	2
Red maraschino cherries, halved	16	16
TOPPING		
Block of light cream cheese, softened	4 oz.	125 g
Icing (confectioner's) sugar	3 tbsp.	50 mL
Light mayonnaise	1/4 cup	60 mL
Chopped salted peanuts	1/4 cup	60 mL
Finely chopped red maraschino cherries	2 tbsp.	30 mL

Dissolve jelly powder in boiling water in medium bowl. Add reserved pear juice and water. Stir. Chill for about 1 hour, stirring and scraping down sides of bowl occasionally, until syrupy.

Add pears, banana and cherries. Stir. Pour into ungreased 9 × 9 inch (22 × 22 cm) pan. Chill until set.

Topping: Beat cream cheese, icing sugar and mayonnaise together well in small bowl. Add peanuts and cherries. Stir. Makes 1 cup (250 mL) topping. Spread evenly over salad. Cuts into 9 pieces.

1 piece: 217 Calories; 7.2 g Total Fat; 229 mg Sodium; 4 g Protein; 36 g Carbohydrate; 2 g Dietary Fiber

Pictured on page 126.

 To store cheese, keep between 35 to 40°F (1.7 to 4.4°C). In the refrigerator, the cheese compartment would normally reflect this temperature range.

Muenster Leeks

*Delicate, slightly sweet leeks are made even more delicious with
mild Muenster cheese and a hint of wine.*

Medium leeks (white and tender parts only)	6	6
Hard margarine (or butter)	2 tbsp.	30 mL
Water	2 tbsp.	30 mL
White (or alcohol-free) wine	2 tbsp.	30 mL
Freshly ground pepper, sprinkle		
Grated Muenster cheese	1 1/2 cups	375 mL
Chopped fresh parsley (or 1/2 tsp., 2 mL, flakes)	2 tsp.	10 mL
Chopped fresh oregano leaves (or 1/2 tsp., 2 mL, dried)	2 tsp.	10 mL
Paprika, sprinkle		

Cut leeks in half lengthwise. Clean well under running water to remove sand and grit.

Lay leeks, curved side down, in greased 2 1/2 quart (2.5 L) shallow casserole or baking dish. Dab here and there with margarine. Drizzle water and wine over leeks. Sprinkle pepper over top. Cover tightly with foil. Bake in 400°F (205°C) oven for 20 minutes. Remove foil. Bake, uncovered, for about 10 minutes until leeks are soft and liquid is mostly evaporated.

Sprinkle cheese, parsley, oregano and paprika over top. Bake for about 10 minutes until cheese is melted and bubbly. Serves 6.

1 serving: 198 Calories; 9.4 g Total Fat; 258 mg Sodium; 9 g Protein; 18 g Carbohydrate; 3 g Dietary Fiber

Pictured on page 143.

 To shred, grate or slice cheese easily, chill cheese until cold. Grate about 4 oz. (113 g) cheese to produce about 1 cup (250 mL) grated cheese.

Eggplant With Greek Cheeses

Individual slices make for easy serving.

SAUCE		
Chopped onion	1 cup	250 mL
Garlic cloves, minced (or 1/2 tsp., 2 mL, powder), optional	2	2
Olive (or cooking) oil	2 tsp.	10 mL
Can of roma (plum) tomatoes, with juice	14 oz.	398 mL
Dried whole oregano	1/2 tsp.	2 mL
Granulated sugar	1/4 tsp.	1 mL
Salt, sprinkle		
Pepper, sprinkle		
Small eggplants, with peel, cut into 1/2 inch (12 mm) thick slices (about 1 1/2 lbs., 680 g)	2	2
Salt	1 tbsp.	15 mL
All-purpose flour	1/2 cup	125 mL
Dried whole oregano	2 tsp.	10 mL
Garlic powder	1 tsp.	5 mL
Pepper	1/2 tsp.	2 mL
Large eggs	3	3
Fine dry bread crumbs	1 cup	250 mL
Olive (or cooking) oil	1/3 cup	75 mL
Greek Kefalotyri (or kasseri) cheese, sliced	8 oz.	225 g
Feta cheese, crumbled (about 3/4 cup, 175 mL)	4 oz.	113 g

Sauce: Sauté onion and garlic in first amount of olive oil in medium frying pan until soft.

Process tomatoes with juice in blender until smooth. Add to onion mixture.

Add first amount of oregano and sugar. Stir. Bring to a boil. Reduce heat. Simmer, uncovered, for 20 minutes, stirring occasionally, until thickened.

Add first amounts of salt and pepper. Set aside. Makes 1 2/3 cups (400 mL) sauce.

Place eggplant in large colander. Sprinkle with second amount of salt. Let drain for 20 minutes. Rinse well.

(continued on next page)

Combine next 4 ingredients in small bowl.

Fork-beat eggs in separate small bowl.

Place bread crumbs in shallow dish. Press eggplant into flour mixture to coat. Dip into egg. Press into bread crumbs to coat.

Cook eggplant, in batches, in second amount of olive oil in large frying pan on medium-high for about 3 minutes per side until crumbs are browned.

Lay eggplant, overlapping, in greased shallow 3 quart (3 L) casserole. Insert Kefalotyri cheese slices between eggplant slices. Drizzle sauce over top.

Sprinkle feta cheese over sauce. Cover. Bake in 350°F (175°C) oven for 45 to 60 minutes until eggplant is tender. Serves 6.

1 serving: 524 Calories; 33.6 g Total Fat; 1899 mg Sodium; 20 g Protein; 37 g Carbohydrate; 2 g Dietary Fiber

Eggplant Parmesan

Lots of sauce and bubbly cheese. Serve with pasta for a main course dish.

Medium eggplants, peeled and cut into 1/2 inch (12 mm) thick slices (about 2 lbs., 900 g)	2	2
Salt, sprinkle		
Cans of tomato sauce (7 1/2 oz., 213 mL, each)	2	2
Dried sweet basil	1 tsp.	5 mL
Dried whole oregano	1/2 tsp.	2 mL
Granulated sugar	1/2 tsp.	2 mL
Grated mozzarella cheese	2 cups	500 mL
Grated Parmesan cheese	1/2 cup	125 mL

Place eggplant in large colander. Lightly sprinkle with salt. Let drain for 20 minutes. Rinse well. Pat dry. Arrange 1/2 of eggplant on broiler pan. Broil for about 5 minutes per side until browned. Repeat with remaining slices.

Combine next 4 ingredients in small bowl. Spread 1/4 cup (60 mL) sauce in bottom of ungreased 2 quart (2 L) casserole. Layer with 1/2 of eggplant. Top with 2/3 cup (150 mL) sauce.

Sprinkle 1/2 of mozzarella and Parmesan cheeses over top. Repeat layers with remaining eggplant, sauce and cheese. Cover. Bake in 400°F (205°C) oven for 35 to 40 minutes until eggplant is tender. Remove cover. Bake for 5 minutes until golden. Serves 6.

1 serving: 221 Calories; 12 g Total Fat; 768 mg Sodium; 14 g Protein; 16 g Carbohydrate; 1 g Dietary Fiber

Pictured on page 143.

Cheese Soufflé

Have everyone seated at the table as you carry in this masterpiece.

Milk	1 cup	250 mL
All-purpose flour	1/4 cup	60 mL
Salt	1/8 tsp.	0.5 mL
Pepper	1/4 tsp.	1 mL
Grated sharp Cheddar cheese	1 cup	250 mL
Egg whites (large), room temperature	4	4
Cream of tartar	1/2 tsp.	2 mL
Egg yolks (large)	4	4
Hot water		

Stir milk into flour, salt and pepper in large saucepan until smooth. Heat and stir on medium until boiling and thickened.

Add cheese. Stir until melted. Remove from heat. Let stand for 30 minutes.

Beat egg whites and cream of tartar in medium bowl until stiff peaks form.

Beat egg yolks in small bowl. Beat into cheese mixture. Fold egg whites into cheese mixture. Turn into ungreased 1 1/2 quart (1.5 L) casserole. Place casserole in larger baking pan. Slowly pour enough boiling water into pan until water comes halfway up sides of casserole. Bake in 325°F (160°C) oven for 45 minutes, without opening oven door for at least first 30 minutes, until golden and firm to touch. Serve immediately. Serves 4 to 6.

1 serving: 253 Calories; 15.7 g Total Fat; 358 mg Sodium; 17 g Protein; 11 g Carbohydrate; trace Dietary Fiber

Scalloped Corn

Sweet corn with scrumptious cheese taste!

Cans of cream-style corn (14 oz., 398 mL, each)	2	2
Large eggs, fork-beaten	2	2
Grated sharp Cheddar cheese	2 cups	500 mL
Soda cracker crumbs	1 cup	250 mL
Salt	1/8 tsp.	0.5 mL
Pepper	1/8 tsp.	0.5 mL
Garlic powder	1/4 tsp.	1 mL

(continued on next page)

134 Side Dishes

Combine all 7 ingredients in ungreased 2 quart (2 L) casserole. Stir well. Bake, uncovered, in 350°F (175°C) oven for 45 to 50 minutes until golden. Makes 4 1/2 cups (1.1 L).

1/2 cup (125 mL): 234 Calories; 11.4 g Total Fat; 609 mg Sodium; 11 g Protein; 25 g Carbohydrate; 2 g Dietary Fiber

Tasty Cornmeal Side Dish

Creamy, soft texture hides cornmeal flavor with a little bite!

Medium onion, finely chopped	1	1
Hard margarine (or butter)	2 tbsp.	30 mL
Diced red pepper	2/3 cup	150 mL
Yellow cornmeal	1 cup	250 mL
Salt	1/2 tsp.	2 mL
Dried crushed chilies	1/4 tsp.	1 mL
Pepper	1/8 tsp.	0.5 mL
Hot water	3 cups	750 mL
Milk	2 cups	500 mL
Grated Monterey Jack With Jalapeño cheese	2 cups	500 mL
Grated sharp Cheddar cheese	1 cup	250 mL
Large eggs, fork-beaten	2	2

Sauté onion in margarine in large saucepan for about 5 minutes until very soft.

Add red pepper. Cook for 2 minutes.

Add cornmeal, salt, chilies and pepper. Slowly stir in hot water and milk until smooth. Heat and stir on medium-low for about 5 minutes until thick porridge-like consistency. Remove from heat.

Add both cheeses. Stir until melted. Fold in eggs. Turn into greased 2 quart (2 L) casserole. Bake, uncovered, in 350°F (175°C) oven for about 45 minutes until puffed and golden. Makes 6 1/2 cups (1.6 L).

3/4 cup (175 mL): 255 Calories; 15.3 g Total Fat; 388 mg Sodium; 13 g Protein; 16 g Carbohydrate; 1 g Dietary Fiber

Basic Cheese Sauce

Serve this thick sauce on tender-crisp cooked vegetables. Broccoli and green beans are transformed into tasty delights that even small children will enjoy!

Hard margarine (or butter)	2 tbsp.	30 mL
All-purpose flour	2 tbsp.	30 mL
Milk	1 1/3 cups	325 mL
Seasoned salt	1/2 tsp.	2 mL
Garlic powder (optional)	1/8 tsp.	0.5 mL
Onion powder	1/8 tsp.	0.5 mL
Paprika	1/8 tsp.	0.5 mL
Cayenne pepper, sprinkle		
Grated medium Cheddar cheese	1 1/2 cups	375 mL

Melt margarine in medium saucepan on medium-low. Stir in flour for about 2 minutes until paste-like consistency. Increase heat to medium.

Gradually stir in milk until boiling and thickened.

Add remaining 6 ingredients. Heat and stir until cheese is melted. Add up to 1/3 cup (75 mL) more milk if a thinner sauce is desired. Makes 1 2/3 cups (400 mL).

2 tbsp. (30 mL): 85 Calories; 6.5 g Total Fat; 161 mg Sodium; 4 g Protein; 2 g Carbohydrate; trace Dietary Fiber

Variation: Omit Cheddar cheese. Use other flavorful firm cheese such as Gruyère or Swiss cheese. Serve over poached eggs on toast, or substitute the "ends" of several flavors of cheeses (before they go moldy) for a delicious sauce to dip toast into for lunch.

Paré Pointer
Birds, like people, fly south in the winter because it's too far to walk.

Broccoli Au Gratin

Mild tasting with lots of broccoli throughout this golden crumb-topped dish.

Fresh broccoli florets and stems, peeled (or 20 oz., 568 g, frozen)	1 1/2 lbs.	680 g
Water		
Chopped onion	3/4 cup	175 mL
Hard margarine (or butter)	2 tbsp.	30 mL
All-purpose flour	1 1/2 tbsp.	25 mL
Milk	1/2 cup	125 mL
Grated mild Cheddar cheese	1 cup	250 mL
Large eggs	2	2
TOPPING		
Hard margarine (or butter)	2 tbsp.	30 mL
Fine dry bread crumbs	1/3 cup	75 mL
Grated medium Cheddar cheese	1/3 cup	75 mL

Cook broccoli in water in large saucepan for 2 to 3 minutes until bright green. Rinse in cold water. Drain. Chop.

Sauté onion in margarine in frying pan until soft and clear.

Sprinkle flour over onion. Mix. Gradually stir in milk until boiling and thickened. Add cheese. Stir until melted.

Beat eggs in medium bowl until frothy. Add broccoli. Stir. Add onion mixture. Stir. Turn into ungreased 2 quart (2 L) casserole.

Topping: Melt margarine in small saucepan. Stir in bread crumbs and cheese until well mixed. Sprinkle over onion mixture. Bake, uncovered, in 350°F (175°C) oven for 40 to 45 minutes until golden. Serves 6.

1 serving: 282 Calories; 19.2 g Total Fat; 372 mg Sodium; 14 g Protein; 16 g Carbohydrate; 3 g Dietary Fiber

 To prevent cheese from losing moisture, one way is to keep cheese wrapped in waxed paper and place in a loose-fitting resealable plastic bag.

Romano Potatoes

Soft, golden brown french fry-like potatoes sprinkled with Romano cheese.

Medium potatoes, peeled and cut into 1/2 inch (12 mm) thick fingers	4	4
Cooking oil	1 1/2 tbsp.	25 mL
Water	1 tbsp.	15 mL
Salt	1 tsp.	5 mL
Grated Romano cheese	3/4 cup	175 mL
Salt, sprinkle (optional)		

Toss potato with cooking oil, water and salt in large bowl. Arrange in single layer on greased baking sheet. Bake in 475°F (240°C) oven for 15 minutes.

Sprinkle cheese over top. Bake for 15 minutes until cheese is golden and potato is tender.

Sprinkle with salt. Serves 4.

1 serving: 211 Calories; 10.7 g Total Fat; 838 mg Sodium; 9 g Protein; 21 g Carbohydrate; 2 g Dietary Fiber

Pictured on page 143.

Parmesan Cauliflower Toss

Fresh Parmesan gives a wonderful flavor to cauliflower.
Vary the amount of cheese to suit your personal taste.

Medium head of cauliflower, trimmed and cut up (about 1 1/2 lbs., 680 g)	1	1
Water		
Salt	1/2 tsp.	2 mL
Hard margarine (or butter)	2 tbsp.	30 mL
Finely grated Parmesan cheese	1/4 – 1/2 cup	60 – 125 mL

Cook cauliflower in water and salt in large saucepan for about 8 minutes until tender. Drain well.

Add margarine and Parmesan cheese. Toss until margarine is melted. Makes 4 cups (1 L). Serves 4 to 6.

1 serving: 125 Calories; 8.2 g Total Fat; 243 mg Sodium; 6 g Protein; 9 g Carbohydrate; 3 g Dietary Fiber

Fast Hash Bake

Baked with two kinds of cheese—this is quick and easy.

Frozen hash brown potatoes	2 1/4 lbs.	1 kg
Milk	2 cups	500 mL
Hard margarine (or butter)	2 tbsp.	30 mL
Process cheese spread	1 cup	250 mL
Grated medium Cheddar cheese	1 cup	250 mL
Garlic powder	1/4 tsp.	1 mL

Put potatoes into greased 9 x 13 inch (22 x 33 cm) pan. Spread evenly.

Combine remaining 5 ingredients in medium saucepan. Heat and stir until cheese is melted. Pour over potatoes. Poke with fork in about 6 spots to help sauce to penetrate. Let stand for 1 hour. Bake in 350°F (175°C) oven for about 1 hour until golden. Serves 10.

1 serving: 250 Calories; 13.1 g Total Fat; 583 mg Sodium; 11 g Protein; 23 g Carbohydrate; 2 g Dietary Fiber

Cheese-Stuffed Potatoes

Good and healthy. Sprinkle with grated Cheddar cheese, if desired.

Medium potatoes, baked	6	6
Hard margarine (or butter), softened	1/4 cup	60 mL
Creamed cottage cheese	1 cup	250 mL
Milk	1/4 cup	60 mL
Minced onion flakes	2 tsp.	10 mL
Salt	1/2 – 1 tsp.	2 – 5 mL
Pepper	1/8 tsp.	0.5 mL

Cut 1/4 inch (6 mm) lengthwise piece from top of each potato. Scoop out pulp, from both tops and bottoms of 2 potatoes, into medium bowl, leaving 1/4 inch (6 mm) thick shells. Discard tops once pulp is removed. Place bottom shells in 9 x 13 (22 x 33 cm) pan.

Add remaining 6 ingredients to pulp. Mash. Divide and stuff into shells. Bake in 400°F (205°C) oven for about 15 minutes until heated through. Makes 6 stuffed potatoes.

1 stuffed potato: 337 Calories; 10.1 g Total Fat; 464 mg Sodium; 10 g Protein; 53 g Carbohydrate; 5 g Dietary Fiber

Rice And Cheese Casserole

Oka is a well established Canadian cheese that takes on a nippier bite as it ages. The almonds add a nice crunch. Mild mushroom and cheese taste.

Medium onion, chopped	1	1
Cooking oil	2 tsp.	10 mL
Long grain white rice, uncooked	1 cup	250 mL
Slivered almonds	1/2 cup	125 mL
Sliced fresh mushrooms (or 10 oz., 284 mL, can, drained)	1 1/2 cups	375 mL
Grated Oka cheese	2 cups	500 mL
Boiling water	2 cups	500 mL
Chicken bouillon powder	1 tbsp.	15 mL

Sauté onion in cooking oil in frying pan until soft. Turn into ungreased 2 quart (2 L) casserole.

Add rice, almonds, mushrooms and cheese. Stir.

Combine boiling water and bouillon powder in liquid measure. Stir to dissolve. Pour over rice mixture. Cover. Bake in 325°F (160°C) oven for about 1 hour until rice is tender and liquid is absorbed. Makes 6 cups (1.5 L). Serves 6.

1 serving: 377 Calories; 21.3 g Total Fat; 576 mg Sodium; 15 g Protein; 32 g Carbohydrate; 2 g Dietary Fiber

Pictured on page 143.

Freezing cheese will almost invariably change the texture. Hard cheese tends to get crumbly and soft cheese separates. For this reason, it is best to use frozen cheese for cooking only. Freezing soft cheese such as cream cheese is best avoided all together because it turns watery and grainy in texture.

Creamed Onion Soup

Very rich soup. Serve with Mom's Cheese Biscuits, page 30.

Day-old thick French bread slices	2	2
Coarsely chopped sweet onion (such as Vidalia or Walla Walla)	4 cups	1 L
Hard margarine (or butter)	1/4 cup	60 mL
Can of condensed beef consommé	10 oz.	284 mL
Water	1 cup	250 mL
Dry white (or alcohol-free) wine	1/3 cup	75 mL
Bay leaf	1	1
Coarsely ground pepper	1/4 tsp.	1 mL
Homogenized milk (or half-and-half cream)	1 1/2 cups	375 mL
All-purpose flour	3 tbsp.	50 mL
Grated nutmeg, sprinkle		
Grated Appenzeller Swiss cheese	1 cup	250 mL
Grated Appenzeller Swiss cheese	1 1/3 cups	325 mL

Cut bread slices into large cubes, about 6 per slice, trying to leave some crust on every piece. Arrange bread cubes in single layer on large ungreased baking sheet. Broil on center rack in oven until toasted. Turn pieces over. Broil until dry and golden brown on all sides. Cool.

Sauté onion in margarine in large pot or Dutch oven on medium for about 20 minutes, stirring occasionally, until very soft and golden.

Add consommé, water, wine, bay leaf and pepper. Stir. Bring to a boil. Reduce heat. Cover. Simmer for 30 minutes to blend flavors. Do not stir. Discard bay leaf.

Stir milk into flour in small bowl until smooth. Gradually stir into onion mixture until simmering and slightly thickened. Remove from heat.

Add nutmeg and first amount of cheese. Heat and stir until cheese is melted.

Divide soup into four ovenproof soup bowls. Float 3 or 4 toasted bread cubes on each serving. Divide and sprinkle second amount of cheese on top. Bake in 400°F (205°C) oven for 15 minutes until bubbly and golden around edges. Makes 3 1/2 cups (875 mL).

1 cup (250 mL): 659 Calories; 39.8 g Total Fat; 1081 mg Sodium; 32 g Protein; 40 g Carbohydrate; 4 g Dietary Fiber

Pictured on page 144.

Cauliflower Cheese Soup

Great cauliflower and cheese taste. Hint of pepper and nutmeg.
Serve with Cheesy Rounds, page 42.

Coarsely chopped cauliflower	4 cups	1 L
Water	2 cups	500 mL
All-purpose flour	1/4 cup	60 mL
Chicken bouillon powder	1 tbsp.	15 mL
Ground nutmeg (optional)	1/4 tsp.	1 mL
Curry powder	1/8 tsp.	0.5 mL
Salt	1 tsp.	5 mL
Pepper	1/4 tsp.	1 mL
Milk	2 cups	500 mL
Milk	2 1/2 cups	625 mL
Grated medium Cheddar cheese	1 cup	250 mL

Cook cauliflower in water in large saucepan until tender. Do not drain.

Combine next 6 ingredients in large pot or Dutch oven.

Stir in first amount of milk until smooth. Heat and stir until boiling and thickened.

Stir in second amount of milk and cauliflower with liquid. Heat, stirring often, until simmering.

Add cheese. Heat and stir until melted. Makes 8 cups (2 L).

1 cup (250 mL): 153 Calories; 6.8 g Total Fat; 722 mg Sodium; 10 g Protein; 13 g Carbohydrate; 1 g Dietary Fiber

1. Eggplant Parmesan, page 133
2. Romano Potatoes, page 138
3. Muenster Leeks, page 131
4. Rice And Cheese Casserole, page 140

Broccoli Cheese Soup

A pretty sage green soup with great broccoli flavor. Not overly rich.
Quick to make. Serve with Feta Dill Biscuits, page 28.

Medium onion, finely chopped	1	1
Hard margarine (or butter)	1 tbsp.	15 mL
Water	2 cups	500 mL
Fresh broccoli florets and stems peeled, cut up (about 4 1/2 cups, 1.1 L)	1 lb.	454 g
Chicken bouillon powder	1 1/2 tbsp.	25 mL
Granulated sugar	1 tsp.	5 mL
Salt	1/4 tsp.	1 mL
Pepper	1/8 tsp.	0.5 mL
Milk	2 1/2 cups	625 mL
Grated medium Cheddar (or Gruyère) cheese	1 cup	250 mL

Sauté onion in margarine in large saucepan until soft.

Add next 6 ingredients. Cover. Cook for about 10 minutes until broccoli is tender. Do not drain. Cool slightly. Transfer to blender in batches. Process until puréed. Return to saucepan.

Add milk and cheese. Stir until hot and cheese is melted. Makes 6 cups (1.5 L).

1 cup (250 mL): 179 Calories; 10.3 g Total Fat; 806 mg Sodium; 11 g Protein; 12 g Carbohydrate; 2 g Dietary Fiber

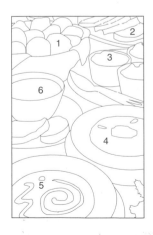

1. Feta Dill Biscuits, page 28
2. Savory Cheese Bread, page 29
3. Creamed Onion Soup, page 141
4. Cheddar Chicken Soup, page 148
5. Cheesy Spinach Soup, page 147
6. Curried Cheese Soup, page 146

Props Courtesy Of: Cherison Enterprises Inc.

Curried Cheese Soup

Mild curry flavor. Serve hot with sandwiches or cold as a starter appetizer.

Cans of condensed beef consommé (10 oz., 284 mL, each)	2	2
Cream cheese, cut up	12 oz.	375 g
Curry paste	1 – 1 1/2 tsp.	5 – 7 mL
Garlic powder	1/8 tsp.	0.5 mL
Paprika	1/4 tsp.	1 mL
Paprika, sprinkle, for garnish		

Put first 5 ingredients into blender. Process until smooth. Heat in saucepan to serve hot or chill to serve cold. If chilled, soup tends to firm up. Stir vigorously with spoon before pouring into individual bowls.

Sprinkle paprika over individual servings. Makes 4 cups (1 L).

1 cup (250 mL): 354 Calories; 34 g Total Fat; 1217 mg Sodium; 10 g Protein; 3 g Carbohydrate; trace Dietary Fiber

Pictured on page 144.

Veggie Cheese Soup

Light orange color with veggie flecks throughout. Smooth, mellow cheese flavor.
Serve with Savory Cheese Bread, page 29.

Grated potato	1/2 cup	125 mL
Grated carrot	1/2 cup	125 mL
Finely chopped onion	1/2 cup	125 mL
Finely chopped celery	1/4 cup	60 mL
Water	2 cups	500 mL
Milk	3 cups	750 mL
Salt	1/2 tsp.	2 mL
Pepper	1/8 tsp.	0.5 mL
Chicken bouillon powder	2 tsp.	10 mL
Milk	1/4 cup	60 mL
All-purpose flour	1/4 cup	60 mL
Grated medium Cheddar cheese	1 1/2 cups	375 mL

(continued on next page)

Combine first 5 ingredients in large pot or Dutch oven. Bring to a boil. Reduce heat. Simmer, uncovered, for 5 minutes until vegetables are tender. Do not drain.

Add first amount of milk, salt, pepper and bouillon powder. Stir. Bring to a boil.

Stir second amount of milk into flour in small cup until smooth. Gradually stir into vegetable mixture until boiling and thickened.

Add cheese. Stir until melted. Serve immediately. Makes 6 1/2 cups (1.6 L).

1 cup (250 mL): 206 Calories; 10.8 g Total Fat; 627 mg Sodium; 12 g Protein; 15 g Carbohydrate; 1 g Dietary Fiber

---

Cheesy Spinach Soup

Wonderful! Vibrant contrast of forest green and white in this wonderfully rich textured soup. Try with Mom's Cheese Biscuits, page 30.

Boxes of frozen chopped spinach (10 oz., 300 g, each), thawed, not drained	2	2
Water	1 cup	250 mL
Milk	1 1/2 cups	375 mL
Water	1/2 cup	125 mL
Chicken bouillon powder	2 tsp.	10 mL
Garlic powder	1/4 tsp.	1 mL
Ground nutmeg	1/4 tsp.	1 mL
Salt	1 tsp.	5 mL
Pepper	1/8 tsp.	0.5 mL
Milk	1/2 cup	125 mL
All-purpose flour	1/4 cup	60 mL
Grated Gruyère cheese	1 1/2 cups	375 mL
Sour cream, for garnish	2 tbsp.	30 mL

Put spinach and first amount of water into blender. Process until smooth. Pour into large saucepan.

Add next 7 ingredients. Heat on medium, stirring often, until simmering.

Stir second amount of milk into flour in small bowl until smooth. Gradually stir into spinach mixture until boiling and thickened.

Add cheese. Stir until melted.

Place dab of sour cream on individual servings. Makes 6 1/2 cups (1.6 L).

1 cup (250 mL): 177 Calories; 9.8 g Total Fat; 731 mg Sodium; 13 g Protein; 10 g Carbohydrate; 2 g Dietary Fiber

Pictured on page 144.

Cheddar Chicken Soup

Orange-colored with a cheese and chicken flavor. Nice consistency.
Serve with Feta Dill Biscuits, page 28.

Grated potato	1/2 cup	125 mL
Grated carrot	3/4 cup	175 mL
Finely diced celery	1/4 cup	60 mL
Finely diced onion	1/4 cup	60 mL
Chicken bouillon powder	1 tbsp.	15 mL
Water	2 1/2 cups	625 mL
Diced cooked chicken	2 cups	500 mL
Steak sauce	1 tsp.	5 mL
Milk	1 cup	250 mL
Milk	1/2 cup	125 mL
All-purpose flour	1/4 cup	60 mL
Salt	1/2 tsp.	2 mL
Pepper	1/8 tsp.	0.5 mL
Grated sharp Cheddar cheese	2 cups	500 mL

Sour cream, for garnish
Chopped fresh chives, for garnish

Put first 6 ingredients into large saucepan. Stir. Bring to a boil. Reduce heat. Simmer, uncovered, for about 5 minutes until vegetables are tender.

Add chicken, steak sauce and first amount of milk. Bring to a boil. Reduce heat to medium.

Stir second amount of milk into flour, salt and pepper in small bowl until smooth. Gradually stir into vegetable mixture until boiling and slightly thickened.

Add cheese. Heat and stir on medium-low until melted. Do not boil.

Place dab of sour cream on individual servings. Sprinkle with chives. Makes 6 1/2 cups (1.6 L).

1 cup (250 mL): 281 Calories; 14.1 g Total Fat; 762 mg Sodium; 26 g Protein; 12 g Carbohydrate; 1 g Dietary Fiber

Pictured on page 144.

Measurement Tables

Throughout this book measurements are given in Conventional and Metric measure. To compensate for differences between the two measurements due to rounding, a full metric measure is not always used. The cup used is the standard 8 fluid ounce. Temperature is given in degrees Fahrenheit and Celsius. Baking pan measurements are in inches and centimetres as well as quarts and litres. An exact metric conversion is given below as well as the working equivalent (Metric Standard Measure).

Spoons

Conventional Measure	Metric Exact Conversion Millilitre (mL)	Metric Standard Measure Millilitre (mL)
1/8 teaspoon (tsp.)	0.6 mL	0.5 mL
1/4 teaspoon (tsp.)	1.2 mL	1 mL
1/2 teaspoon (tsp.)	2.4 mL	2 mL
1 teaspoon (tsp.)	4.7 mL	5 mL
2 teaspoons (tsp.)	9.4 mL	10 mL
1 tablespoon (tbsp.)	14.2 mL	15 mL

Cups

Conventional Measure	Metric Exact Conversion Millilitre (mL)	Metric Standard Measure Millilitre (mL)
1/4 cup (4 tbsp.)	56.8 mL	60 mL
1/3 cup (5 1/3 tbsp.)	75.6 mL	75 mL
1/2 cup (8 tbsp.)	113.7 mL	125 mL
2/3 cup (10 2/3 tbsp.)	151.2 mL	150 mL
3/4 cup (12 tbsp.)	170.5 mL	175 mL
1 cup (16 tbsp.)	227.3 mL	250 mL
4 1/2 cups	1022.9 mL	1000 mL (1 L)

Oven Temperatures

Fahrenheit (°F)	Celsius (°C)
175°	80°
200°	95°
225°	110°
250°	120°
275°	140°
300°	150°
325°	160°
350°	175°
375°	190°
400°	205°
425°	220°
450°	230°
475°	240°
500°	260°

Dry Measurements

Conventional Measure Ounces (oz.)	Metric Exact Conversion Grams (g)	Metric Standard Measure Grams (g)
1 oz.	28.3 g	28 g
2 oz.	56.7 g	57 g
3 oz.	85.0 g	85 g
4 oz.	113.4 g	125 g
5 oz.	141.7 g	140 g
6 oz.	170.1 g	170 g
7 oz.	198.4 g	200 g
8 oz.	226.8 g	250 g
16 oz.	453.6 g	500 g
32 oz.	907.2 g	1000 g (1 kg)

Pans

Conventional Inches	Metric Centimetres
8x8 inch	20x20 cm
9x9 inch	22x22 cm
9x13 inch	22x33 cm
10x15 inch	25x38 cm
11x17 inch	28x43 cm
8x2 inch round	20x5 cm
9x2 inch round	22x5 cm
10x4 1/2 inch tube	25x11 cm
8x4x3 inch loaf	20x10x7.5 cm
9x5x3 inch loaf	22x12.5x7.5 cm

Casseroles

CANADA & BRITAIN		UNITED STATES	
Standard Size Casserole	Exact Metric Measure	Standard Size Casserole	Exact Metric Measure
1 qt. (5 cups)	1.13 L	1 qt. (4 cups)	900 mL
1 1/2 qts. (7 1/2 cups)	1.69 L	1 1/2 qts. (6 cups)	1.35 L
2 qts. (10 cups)	2.25 L	2 qts. (8 cups)	1.8 L
2 1/2 qts. (12 1/2 cups)	2.81 L	2 1/2 qts. (10 cups)	2.25 L
3 qts. (15 cups)	3.38 L	3 qts. (12 cups)	2.7 L
4 qts. (20 cups)	4.5 L	4 qts. (16 cups)	3.6 L
5 qts. (25 cups)	5.63 L	5 qts. (20 cups)	4.5 L

Photo Index

Tip Index

Cheese Index

Recipe Index

155

156

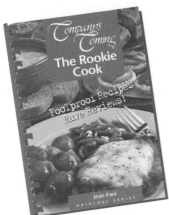

The Rookie Cook

New July 1, 2002

The Rookie Cook has easy-to-make, yet impressive, recipes that will build confidence in the beginner chef. Rave reviews are in the making!

Pecan Chip Cookies

Lots of pecans and chocolate chips in these delicious cookies. Be sure not to overbake so they stay soft.

Hard margarine (or butter), softened	1 cup	250 mL
Brown sugar, packed	1 1/2 cups	375 mL
Granulated sugar	1/2 cup	125 mL
Large eggs	2	2
Vanilla	1 1/2 tsp.	7 mL
All-purpose flour	2 1/2 cups	625 mL
Baking powder	1 tsp.	5 mL
Baking soda	1 tsp.	5 mL
Salt	1/2 tsp.	2 mL
Semisweet chocolate chips	2 cups	500 mL
Chopped pecans	1 cup	250 mL

Cream margarine and both sugars together in large bowl until light and fluffy. Add eggs, 1 at a time, beating well after each addition. Add vanilla. Beat well.

Combine flour, baking powder, baking soda and salt in medium bowl. Add to margarine mixture. Mix until no dry flour remains and stiff dough forms.

Add chocolate chips and pecans. Stir until evenly distributed. Drop by tablespoonfuls, 2 to 3 inches (5 to 7.5 cm) apart, onto greased cookie sheets. Bake in 350°F (175°C) oven for 10 minutes until edges are golden. Do not overbake. Let stand on cookie sheets for 3 minutes before removing to wire racks to cool. Makes 7 dozen cookies.

1 cookie: 87 Calories; 4.7 g Total Fat; 64 mg Sodium; 1 g Protein; 11 g Carbohydrate; trace Dietary Fiber

Company's Coming cookbooks are available at retail locations throughout Canada!

See mail order form

Buy any 2 cookbooks—choose a 3rd FREE of equal or less value than the lowest price paid.   *Available in French

Original Series	CA$14.99 Canada		US$10.99 USA & International	
CODE		**CODE**		**CODE**
SQ	150 Delicious Squares*	LR	Light Recipes*	MAM	Make-Ahead Meals*
CA	Casseroles*	PR	Preserves*	PB	The Potato Book*
MU	Muffins & More*	LCA	Light Casseroles*	CCLFC	Low-Fat Cooking*
SA	Salads*	CH	Chicken*	CCLFP	Low-Fat Pasta*
AP	Appetizers	KC	Kids Cooking	AC	Appliance Cooking*
DE	Desserts	BR	Breads*	CFK	Cook For Kids
SS	Soups & Sandwiches	ME	Meatless Cooking*	SCH	Stews, Chilies & Chow
CO	Cookies*	CT	Cooking For Two*	FD	Fondues
VE	Vegetables	BB	Breakfasts & Brunches*	CCBE	The Beef Book
MC	Main Courses	SC	Slow Cooker Recipes*	ASI	Asian Cooking
PA	Pasta*	PZ	Pizza*	CB	The Cheese Book
CK	Cakes	ODM	One Dish Meals*	RC	The Rookie Cook ◀NE
BA	Barbecues*	ST	Starters*		*July 1/02*
PI	Pies*	SF	Stir-Fry*		

Greatest Hits	CA$12.99 Canada		US$9.99 USA & International	
CODE		**CODE**		**CODE**
BML	Biscuits, Muffins & Loaves*	SAS	Soups & Salads*	ITAL	Italian
DSD	Dips, Spreads & Dressings*	SAW	Sandwiches & Wraps*	MEX	Mexican

Lifestyle Series	CA$16.99 Canada	US$12.99 USA & International
CODE		
GR	Grilling*	
DC	Diabetic Cooking*	

Special Occasion Series	CA$19.99 Canada	US$19.99 USA & International
CODE		**CODE**
CE	Chocolate Everything*	CFS	Cooking for the Seasons
GFK	Gifts from the Kitchen		

Company's Coming COOKBOOKS

www.companyscoming.com
visit our web-site

COMPANY'S COMING PUBLISHING LIMITED
2311 - 96 Street
Edmonton, Alberta, Canada T6N 1G3
Tel: (780) 450-6223 Fax: (780) 450-1857

Exclusive Mail Order Offer

See page 158 for list of cookbooks

Buy 2 Get 1 FREE!
Buy any 2 cookbooks—choose a 3rd FREE of equal or less value than the lowest price paid.

Quantity	Code	Title	Price Each	Price Total
			$	$
		don't forget		
		to indicate your		
		free book(s).		
		(see exclusive mail order		
		offer above)		
		please print		
	TOTAL BOOKS (including FREE)	TOTAL BOOKS PURCHASED:	$	

	International		Canada & USA	
Plus Shipping & Handling (per destination)	$7.00	(one book)	$5.00	(1-3 books)
Additional Books (including FREE books)	$	($2.00 each)	$	($1.00 each)
Sub-Total	$		$	
Canadian residents add G.S.T(7%)			$	
TOTAL AMOUNT ENCLOSED	$		$	

The Fine Print

- Orders outside Canada must be **PAID IN US FUNDS** by cheque or money order drawn on Canadian or US bank or by credit card.
- Make cheque or money order payable to: **COMPANY'S COMING PUBLISHING LIMITED**.
- Prices are expressed in Canadian dollars for Canada, US dollars for USA & International and are subject to change without prior notice.
- Orders are shipped surface mail. For courier rates, visit our web-site: **www.companyscoming.com** or contact us: **Tel: (780) 450-6223 Fax: (780) 450-1857.**
- Sorry, no C.O.D's.

Gift Giving

- Let us help you with your gift giving!
- We will send cookbooks directly to the recipients of your choice if you give us their names and addresses.
- Please specify the titles you wish to send to each person.
- If you would like to include your personal note or card, we will be pleased to enclose it with your gift order.
- Company's Coming Cookbooks make excellent gifts: Birthdays, bridal showers, Mother's Day, Father's Day, graduation or any occasion...collect them all!

☐ MasterCard ☐ VISA

_____
Expiry date

Account # _____

Name of cardholder _____

Cardholder's signature _____

Shipping Address
Send the cookbooks listed above to:

Name: _____

Street: _____

City: _____ Prov./State: _____

Country: _____ Postal Code/Zip: _____

Tel: (_____) _____

E-mail address: _____

☐ YES! Please send a catalogue

Canada's most
popular
cookbooks!